A Princess to the Throne

Mary Jane Clark

A Princess to the Throne
© 2018 by Mary Jane Clark

ISBN: 978-1-63073-246-2

Mary Jane Clark's picture was taken by: Peggy Williams

Published and printed by:
Faithful Life Publishers
North Fort Myers, FL 33903

888.720.0950 • info@FaithfulLifePublishers.com
FaithfulLifePublishers.com

Scripture quotations are from the Authorized King James Version.

Published in the United States of America

22 21 20 19 18   1 2 3 4 5

Table of Contents

Are You a Child of the King?

John 1:10-14, "*10 He was in the world, and the world was made by him, and the world knew him not. 11 He came unto his own, and his own received him not. 12 But as many as received him, to them gave he power to become the sons of God, even to them that believe on his name: 13 Which were born, not of blood, nor of the will of the flesh, nor of the will of man, but of God. 14 And the Word was made flesh, and dwelt among us, (and we beheld his glory, the glory as of the only begotten of the Father,) full of grace and truth.*"

Through Jesus we have the power to become the sons (or daughters) of God. Through Jesus' ministry on Earth, he was very clear on how to become a child of the king. In John 3:3, "*Jesus answered and said unto him, Verily, verily, I say unto thee, Except a man be born again, he cannot see the kingdom of God.*"

Jesus continued to say…

John 3:14-17, "*And as Moses lifted up the serpent in the wilderness, even so must the Son of man be lifted up: 15 That whosoever believeth in him should not perish, but have eternal life. 16 For God so loved the world, that he gave his only begotten Son, that whosoever believeth in him should not perish, but have everlasting life. 17 For God sent not his Son into the world to condemn the world; but that the world through him might be saved."*

God loves you so much that he sent His son to come to earth and die on a cross for your sins. He paid the debt or what your payment would have been for your sins. Jesus died so you could be free from the power of sin.

Jesus said in John 14:6, *"I am the way, the truth and the life no man cometh unto the Father but by me."*

In times of kings, only those who were invited by the king could come into his presence. Jesus told us that the only way into the King's presence was through Him.

"Yes" to the King

God is a gracious King. He gave each of us a free will to choose to be His child or to go our own way. The choice is yours; however, just as He gave His all for you, God wants us to give our all. The Bible tells us in Luke 16:13, *"No servant can serve two masters: for either he will hate the one, and love the other; or else he will hold to the one, and despise the other. Ye cannot serve God and mammon."*

"Mammon" according to *Strong's Concordance* is riches, money, possessions, or property. Some identify it as something that you put your trust in.

What are you putting your trust in?

_____

_____

_____

_____

_____

Read 2 Corinthians 1:18-24

In your own words, what do these verses say?

_____

_____

_____

_____

_____

As you study God's word, each word is important. Some words in this passage that stand out are stablisheth, anointed, and sealed.

Why would these words be important?

Just as the Apostle Paul was stablished or confirmed and anointed by God. We are established as daughters to the King through God by putting our trust in Christ Jesus to save us and give us eternal life. We need to understand that we cannot save ourselves or trust in our own abilities to get to Heaven. Paul was sealed by God, the King of Kings. A seal was often used by a king in Bible times as a "legal signature" which guaranteed the promise (contents) of what was sealed and usually done through the king's signet or ring. Paul's life changed dramatically as a result of putting his faith in God through Christ Jesus. Meeting Christ was a life-changing experience for Paul.

Have you said "Yes" to the King of Kings?

_____

_____

If you have, has your life been changed?

_____

_____

_____

_____

_____

Rags to Riches

Our righteousness (the good things we do) is as filthy rags according to Isaiah 64:6

Read John 12:44-50.

Let's break these verses down to study this portion of scripture.

Vs 44 Whom should we believe on? _____

Vs 45 If we see the character of Jesus, who else do we see?

_____

Vs 46 If we believe in Jesus, what promise is in this verse?

_____

_____

If we have believed in Jesus and have asked Him to be our Savior; we do not have to *"live in darkness."* This is an incredible promise from God's word. This is Jesus speaking in this verse giving us the answers that we need to inherit the kingdom. It is personal. It is not a decision someone else can make for you.

What does Jesus mean by darkness?

_____

_____

Darkness according to *Strong's Concordance* refers to "a brand of moral, spiritual obscurity that is blocking out the light of God when faith is lacking."

Are you living in darkness?

_____

_____

Wednesday:

Who is a Child of the King?

God did not want us to live apart from him; however our sin separates us from a Holy God. Have you trusted Christ to be your Savior? If so, do you know when you trusted Jesus Christ as your Savior?

_____

You do not have to know the exact time, but you should know it happened. God only has children; you have not always been a Christian. Just as there is a time and date for your physical birthday, the Lord told Nicademus that *"ye must be born again"* (John 3:7). Not a physical birth, but a spiritual birth. What does John 3:3 say?

"The wind bloweth where it listeth, and thou hearest the sound thereof, but canst not tell whence it cometh, and whither it goeth: so is every one that is born of the Spirit." John 3:8

This is a time when you realize that you are a sinner and there is nothing you can do to merit heaven. It is a gift of God through Christ, who lived a sinless life, died on the cross for your sins, and had victory over the grave through His resurrection and ascension into heaven.

What is sin?

_____

_____

Do you sin? _____

Romans 3:23 says that we have all sinned. What are some examples of sin?

_____

_____

_____

_____

_____

Even as Christians, who have Christ in our lives, we still sin. What are some areas in your life where you struggle?

Read 1 John 1:8-10.

What does verse 8 and 10 say about sin?

_____

_____

What does verse 9 say about sin?

_____

_____

What sins do you need to confess?

_____

_____

_____

If you have asked Christ to be your Savior, God sees the blood of Jesus Christ that was shed on the cross for your sins. 1 John 2:1-2 says, *"My little children, these things write I unto you, that ye sin not. And if any man sin, we have an advocate with the Father, Jesus Christ the righteous: 2 And he is the propitiation for our sins: and not for ours only, but also for the sins of the whole world."*

According to the *Strong's Concordance*, propitiation is an appeasing sacrifice. Jesus was the sacrifice for God to see past our

11

sins. For this to happen, you have to understand that you are a sinner and you cannot get to heaven on your own merit. You have to believe that Jesus is the Son of God that came to die on the cross for your sin and confess your need of Jesus to be the sacrifice for those sins. Ephesians 2:8-9 says, *"For by grace are ye saved through faith; and that not of yourselves:* [it is] *the gift of God: 9 Not of works, lest any man should boast."*

1 John 5:1 says, *"Whosoever believeth that Jesus is the Christ is born of God: and every one that loveth him that begat loveth him also that is begotten of him."* Then verse 4 says, *"For whatsoever is born of God overcometh the world: and this is the victory that overcometh the world, even our faith."*

When you put your faith and trust in Jesus Christ to be your sacrifice, you become a child of the King of Kings. If you have made this important decision, do you have unconfessed sin in your life? Are there areas of your life that you need to give to God? 1 John 1:9 says, *"If we confess our sins, he is faithful and just to forgive us* [our] *sins, and to cleanse us from all unrighteousness."*

Thursday:

Are You a Daughter of the King?

Have you asked Christ to be your Savior? _____

Romans 5:15, "*But not as the offence, so also is the free gift. For if through the offence of one many be dead, much more the grace of God, and the gift by grace, which is by one man, Jesus Christ, hath abounded unto many.*"

The gift is free. As we look at the rest of the verse,

"*...For if through the offence of one many be dead,*" - Adam's sin separated us from God

"*much more the grace of God,*" -because God is so gracious

"*and the gift by grace*" -God provided a gift because of His grace

"*which is by one man, Jesus Christ,*" -the gift is Jesus Christ

"*hath abounded unto many.*" -overflows to many

Who can receive this free gift?

_____

_____

Have you accepted the gift of God through Jesus Christ noted in John 3:16? A gift does not become yours until you take it. A gift also needs to be opened to enjoy. You can leave a gift wrapped, but you will never get to experience the gift until you open it up, take it out of the box, and use it or look at it. How often do you receive a gift and keep it wrapped up? Most rip into the packages as quickly as possible to see what is inside. The same is true with this wonderful gift from our God, who loves us more than anyone else. He wants you to accept His gift of Jesus, open His Word and find out who Jesus

13

is and experience him for yourself, and enjoy God's presence as never before.

Write out when you accepted the gift of Jesus. If you have, you are a daughter of the King.

_____

_____

_____

_____

_____

Sealed by the King's Ring

Over the years, I have dealt with children and adults from various backgrounds with differing opinions over the issue of losing their salvation. The question is often can you or do you lose your salvation? It is not about what people believe. It is about what God's word says. Let's answer our questions through God's word. This is what God's word says, *"Study to shew thyself approved unto God, a workman that needeth not to be ashamed, rightly dividing the word of truth."* 2 Timothy 2:15. Use scripture to validate scripture. Study God's word to find the answers to your questions. Know what you believe and why you believe it. There are some well-meaning religious groups and Christians who use a man's philosophy above the word of God. So let's check out what God's word says....

John 6:27-29, *"Labour not for the meat which perisheth, but for that meat which endureth unto everlasting life, which the Son of man shall give unto you: for him hath God the Father sealed. 28 Then said they unto him, What shall we do, that we might work the works of God? 29 Jesus answered and said unto them, This is the work of God, that ye believe on him whom he hath sent."*

Ephesians 1:4-7, *"According as he hath chosen us in him before the foundation of the world, that we should be holy and without blame before him in love: 5 Having predestinated us* **unto the adoption** *of children by Jesus Christ to himself, according to the good pleasure of his will, 6 To the praise of the glory of his grace, wherein he hath made us accepted in the beloved. 7 In whom we have redemption through his blood, the forgiveness of sins, according to the riches of his grace;"* [Emphasis added]

Ephesians 1:10-14, *"That in the dispensation of the fulness of times he might gather together in one all things in Christ, both which are in heaven, and which are on earth; even in him: 11In whom also we have* **obtained an inheritance**, *being predestinated according to the purpose of him who worketh all things after the counsel of his own will: 12 That we should be to the praise of his glory, who first trusted in Christ. 13 In whom ye also trusted, after that ye heard the word of truth, the gospel of your salvation: in whom also after that ye believed,* **ye were sealed with that holy Spirit of promise**, *14 Which is the earnest of our inheritance until the redemption of the purchased possession, unto the praise of his glory."* [Emphasis added]

Galatians 4:4-7, *"But when the fulness of the time was come, God sent forth his Son, made of a woman, made under the law, 5 To redeem them that were under the law, that we might* **receive the adoption of sons**. *6 And because ye are sons, God hath sent forth the Spirit of his Son into your hearts, crying, Abba, Father. 7 Wherefore thou art no more a servant, but a son; and if a son, then* **an heir of God** *through Christ."* [Emphasis added]

As you read the verses, emphasis was added on key phrases used in God's word to give you promise and assurance of your inheritance. Some commentaries note that in Bible times, a child that was adopted into a family was chosen and had the same rights as the biological children; however, adoptions in Bible times were sealed and prevented the parents from disowning the child for any reason. They would inherit the full blessing as an heir. The King's seal made it so. His ring authenticated letters, laws, decrees, power, and authority. What man has more authority than God? If you have faith to believe that God can save you, why do we doubt what God's word states about our salvation?

Jesus also provided another example in John 10:26-30, *"But ye believe not, because ye are not of my sheep, as I said unto you. 27 My sheep hear my voice, and I know them, and they follow me: 28 And I give unto them eternal life; and they shall never perish,* **neither shall any man pluck them out of my hand.** *29 My Father, which gave them me, is greater than all; and no man is able to pluck them out of my Father's hand. 30 I and my Father are one."* [Emphasis added] If God's word states that you cannot be plucked out of the hand of the Almighty, whose hand is strong enough to open it? Is it your hand?

How do you know that you know?

_____

_____

_____

_____

_____

Saturday:

Bought with a Price: Remember whose you are?

Is it a free ticket to live your life however you want?

Romans 12:1-3, "*I beseech you therefore, brethren, by the mercies of God, that ye present your bodies a living sacrifice, holy, acceptable unto God, which is your reasonable service. 2 And be not conformed to this world: but be ye transformed by the renewing of your mind, that ye may prove what is that good, and acceptable, and perfect, will of God. 3 For I say, through the grace given unto me, to every man that is among you, not to think of himself more highly than he ought to think; but to think soberly, according as God hath dealt to every man the measure of faith.*"

What do these three verses teach about the grace you have been given?

_____

_____

_____

What does the word sacrifice mean?

_____

_____

_____

Even in Bible times through the adoption process, the adopted child was placed under the authority of the father. The same is true when you became a child of the King. You were placed under the protection, provision, and authority of the King of Kings. You were bought with a price (1 Corinthians 7:23) and Romans 12 tells us that our bodies should be a living sacrifice (an offering that is accepted because it is on His terms), because this is our reasonable (logical to God) service for being bought with a price.

Romans 1:4-6, *"And declared to be the Son of God with power, according to the spirit of holiness, by the resurrection from the dead: 5 By whom we have received grace and apostleship, for obedience to the faith among all nations, **for his name**: 6 Among whom are ye also the called of Jesus Christ:."*

What name do you have now? Are you a daughter of the King?

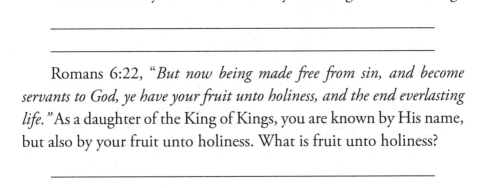

Romans 6:22, *"But now being made free from sin, and become servants to God, ye have your fruit unto holiness, and the end everlasting life."* As a daughter of the King of Kings, you are known by His name, but also by your fruit unto holiness. What is fruit unto holiness?

The word used here is the same word used in Galatians 5:22, *"for the fruit of the Spirit....love, joy, peace, kindness, goodness, gentleness, self-control."* Some commentaries suggest that your fruit unto holiness is sanctification. As we are sanctified (set apart) for God's glory, we are called to be a living sacrifice that is holy and acceptable unto God. Our life should reflect the fruit of our love for our Heavenly Father through our attitudes, words, and deeds. A life yielded to the Father will grow love, joy, peace, kindness, goodness, gentleness, and self-control.

No title of princess comes without obligations and duties to uphold. Throughout this devotional, we will explore your role as a daughter of the King of Kings.

Take some time to honestly reflect on how you represent the King of Kings:

Are you a living sacrifice? _____

How and where do you spend your time?

_____

_____

_____

What kind of fruit do others see in you?

_____

_____

_____

Would God (who is perfect and holy) be pleased with your thoughts and actions? _____

If your friends, parents, pastor, or youth leader wrote an article about you as a princess, what would it include?

_____

_____

_____

_____

_____

Sunday:

The Way to the Kingdom

Sunday is the day of worship in most churches. Today is the day we set apart to study God's word in Sunday school, sing praises to God for His honor and glory, and heed the warnings and discover the truths in God's word through Bible-based preaching. Services in the local church are not meant to be entertainment for Christians (those saved from eternal separation from God through the sacrifice and acceptance of Jesus Christ as the only way to the Father). In preparation for a day of worship, ask God to show you areas of your life that need to be changed, submitted to God, and how to encourage others within the fellowship of believers.

Pray this scripture.

Psalms 139:23, *"Search me, O God, and know my heart: try me, and know my thoughts: And see if there be any wicked way in me, and lead me in the way everlasting."* Be prepared for the Lord to start changing your life.

What did God show me today?

_____

_____

_____

_____

What areas of my life do I need to submit to God?

_____

_____

_____

_____

How can I be a blessing to others or encourage other believers today?

_____

_____

_____

_____

_____

How can I be a blessing to others or encourage others this week?

_____

_____

_____

_____

_____

Learning to be a Princess

My prayer is that each of you has made the decision to be a Princess to the Throne by asking Christ to be your personal Savior. This places you in the royal family. As a believer in the Lord Jesus Christ, your life should begin to change as you learn what it means to be a princess, get to know the royal family, understand the privileges of being part of the royal family, and understand your duties and responsibilities of being in the royal family. Being a princess is hard work, but the rewards are awesome!!

How do you get to know someone?

You might say talk to them, spend time with them, find out their likes and dislikes, and learn about their interests. When someone is your best friend, you want to spend as much time with them as possible, do things that make them happy, and your focus shifts from you to them. Our relationship with God is similar in that while he is your Heavenly Father, he also desires to be your friend. There are many examples in God's word of people who walked close with God in the Old Testament and those who walked with Christ on this Earth in the New Testament.

Monday:

Getting to know the King of Kings

As earlier mentioned, getting to know someone involves spending time with them and finding out about their likes or dislikes. As you get to know the King of Kings, the Bible is our love letter. God used inspired men to provide His children with a tool to get to know Him.

Psalms 119:1-4, *"Blessed are the undefiled in the way, who walk in the law of the LORD. 2 Blessed are they that keep his testimonies, and that seek him with the whole heart. 3 They also do no iniquity: they walk in his ways. 4 Thou hast commanded us to keep thy precepts diligently."*

What does this mean?

Vs 1: *Blessed...who walk in the law-*

_____

_____

Vs 2 *Blessed...keep his testimonies-*

  Who seek with whole heart-

_____

_____

Vs 3 *no iniquity: they walk in his ways-*

_____

_____

Vs 4 *keep thy precepts diligently-*

_____

_____

These verses show us that the law (or God's word) reveals God's desire for you to do what His word says (walk in the law and keep thy precepts) and be a witness (keep His testimonies) for Him, to seek (or search) for His likes and dislikes. Verse 3, *"no iniquity: they walk in his ways"* does not mean that we do not sin, but that our heart reveals our desire to walk in His ways. David in the Bible was a man after God's own heart (Acts 13:22) and walked in the path of the God, but sinned.

Psalms 119:105, *"Thy word is a lamp unto my feet, and a light unto my path. By reading God's word, God will also give us direction for our lives."*

Read Matthew 4:1-4.

What is Jesus saying?

_____

_____

_____

_____

_____

As a daughter to the King, we cannot live on the bread of this earth (food), but it is necessary for us to live by the word of God. This is done through reading God's word and getting to know him. How often do you need physical food?

Proverbs 8:33-36 says, *"Hear instruction, and be wise, and refuse it not. 34 Blessed is the man that heareth me, watching daily at my gates, waiting at the posts of my doors. 35 For whoso findeth me findeth life, and shall obtain favour of the LORD. 36 But he that sinneth against me wrongeth his own soul:..."*

A couple of things found in this verse:

1. One way we hear instruction is through God's word.

2. Are we daily hearing and watching?

3. We know what God calls sin by reading God's word.

May God show His word to you today through the Holy Spirit. Get to know your King by reading His word and learning about your role as a princess.

Tuesday:

Delight Yourself in the Law of the Land

Read Psalms 1.

As a princess, how do you know what is ungodly, or if you are standing with sinners or sitting with the scornful (mocker)? We know this by studying the word of God.

Titus 1:10-16 says, *"For there are many unruly and vain talkers* **and deceivers,** *specially they of the circumcision: 11* **Whose mouths must be stopped,** *who subvert whole houses,* **teaching things which they ought not,** *for filthy lucre's sake. 12 One of themselves, even a prophet of their own, said, The Cretians are alway liars, evil beasts, slow bellies. 13 This witness is true. Wherefore* **rebuke them sharply,** *that they may be sound in the faith; 14 Not giving heed to Jewish fables, and commandments of men, that turn from the truth. 15 Unto the pure all things are pure: but unto them that are defiled and unbelieving is nothing pure; but even their mind and conscience is defiled. 16 They profess that they know God; but in works they deny him, being* **abominable, and disobedient,** *and unto every good work reprobate."* [Emphasis added]

How do we know if we are being deceived, disobedient, or abominable?

2 Timothy 2:14-16, tells us *"Of these things put them in remembrance, charging them before the Lord that they strive not about words to no profit, but to the subverting of the hearers. 15 Study to shew thyself approved unto God, a workman that needeth not to be ashamed, rightly dividing the word of truth. 16 But shun profane and vain babblings: for they will increase unto more ungodliness."* We also should study so we do not shame the King of Kings through our actions. We need to know what God's word says and what it means.

What tools help us to study God's word?

The Holy Spirit is your best guide to understanding scripture. Pray that the Holy Spirit will show you something out of God's word that you can apply to your life or that you might need for today. If you were taking a test on a subject that you did not know anything about; it would be tough. Dig into what God's word says by using scripture to understand scripture. Bible references written in your margins can help or use a Bible Concordance. A dictionary is helpful to look up unfamiliar words or a Bible program such as biblehub.com. Don't settle for merely reading God's word, so you can check it off of your "To-Do" list. Start with one verse. We will practice this throughout the devotional.

Wednesday:

Memorize the Law of the Land

Psalms 119:93-94, *"I will never forget thy precepts: for with them thou hast quickened me. 94 I am thine, save me; for I have sought thy precepts"*

Psalms 119:109, *"My soul is continually in my hand: yet do I not forget thy law."*

Psalms 119:115-116, *"Depart from me, ye evildoers: for I will keep the commandments of my God. 116 Uphold me according unto thy word, that I may live: and let me not be ashamed of my hope."*

How do we not forget? How do we keep the commandments of God?

1. We must read them.

2. We must study them.

3. We must memorize them

Psalms 119:11, *"Thy word have I hid in mine heart, that I might not sin against thee."*

Read Proverbs 2:1-12.

Why is memorization so important?

The Bible says in these verses that it gives wisdom, good judgment, a path, knowledge, discretion, preservation and deliverance from walking in darkness.

Choose a verse that will help you with something in your life.

Which verse did you choose?

_____

_____

Hints: Write it down and read it several times every day, until you know it. Sometimes it helps to write it over and over. Then pick another verse.

_____

_____

_____

_____

_____

_____

_____

_____

_____

Thursday:

Meditate on the King's Love Letter

Psalms 119: 97-99, *"O how love I thy law! it is my meditation all the day. 98 Thou through thy commandments hast made me wiser than mine enemies: for they are ever with me. 99 I have more understanding than all my teachers: for thy testimonies are my meditation."*

Psalms 119:103-104, *"How sweet are thy words unto my taste! yea, sweeter than honey to my mouth! 104 Through thy precepts I get understanding: therefore I hate every false way."*

What does meditate mean?

Meditate is a verb that means to think deeply about. Synonyms for meditate are to contemplate, think, consider, ponder, muse, reflect, deliberate, ruminate, chew the cud, brood, mull something over.

Wow!! How incredible to think of God's word deeply!! Think about the verses above. Do you meditate on God's word? After you read, are you done for the day? Do you reflect and apply the verses God puts before you that day?

Meditate on Psalms 119:103-104 today.

Reflect:

Are God's words sweet unto my taste?

Do I crave God like I crave sweets?

Is God's word sweeter than honey to me? Is the word of God precious to me in my everyday life?

Do I learn and get understanding from God's word?

Do I know false teaching when it is before me to hate it?

How can I apply this verse to my life today?

31

_____

_____

_____

_____

_____

Write this verse out and put it somewhere to see it throughout the day.

Friday:

Talk to the King

Whether you talk, text, email or write a friend, you must talk to this person to get to know them and learn about them. The things they like and dislike change over time. Jesus told us in Luke 18:1, *"And he spake a parable unto them to this end, **that men ought always to pray,** and not to faint;"* [Emphasis added]

While Jesus was on this Earth, He gave us a model prayer and told us that we should pray. He also shared with us the importance of how we pray and the purpose of our prayer.

Matthew 6:5-8, *"And when thou prayest, thou shalt not be as the hypocrites are: for they love to pray standing in the synagogues and in the corners of the streets, that they may be seen of men. Verily I say unto you, They have their reward. 6 But thou, when thou prayest, enter into thy closet, and when thou hast shut thy door, pray to thy Father which is in secret; and thy Father which seeth in secret shall reward thee openly. 7 But when ye pray, use not vain repetitions, as the heathen do: for they think that they shall be heard for their much speaking. 8 Be not ye therefore like unto them: for your Father knoweth what things ye have need of, before ye ask him."*

What do these verses say about prayer?

_____

_____

_____

_____

_____

What is a hypocrite?

_____

_____

What should not be in our prayers?

According to Easton's Bible Dictionary, a hypocrite is "one who puts on a mask and feigns himself to be what he is not; a dissembler in religion." God wants us to be genuine in our prayers, not praying for show as the religious leaders of the time were doing. Their prayers were for men. God knows our heart and our motives behind our prayers. What are vain repetitions? According to *Strong's Concordance*, vain repetitions mean that "I chatter, am long-winded, utter empty words, stammer, and repeat." As we talk to the King of Kings, we need to be genuine and sincere. We also need to pray with faith that God, who saved you from your sins, can answer prayers that are according to His will and will bring honor and glory to Him.

Read John 14:5-13.

1 John 5:13-15 *"These things have I written unto you that believe on the name of the Son of God; that ye may know that ye have eternal life, and that ye may believe on the name of the Son of God. 14 And this is the confidence that we have in him, that, if we ask any thing according to his will, he heareth us: 15 And if we know that he hear us, whatsoever we ask, we know that we have the petitions that we desired of him."*

The King is not going to grant a petition (or prayer) that is against His laws. A princess knows the laws of the land and delights in keeping His commandments; therefore she would be thoughtful in her petitions to the King.

Saturday:

Listen to the King's Direction

Read Psalms 81: 8-13.

These verses talk about the importance of listening to the King's direction in the life of Israel. The same is true for the daughter of the King.

Verse 8, *"Hear, O my people,... hearken unto me;"* Verse 10, *"I am the LORD thy God..."* Verse 11, *"But my people would not hearken to my voice; and Israel would none of me."* Israel did not listen to the voice of the King of Kings. The Psalm says in Verse 12 that, *"So I gave them up unto their own hearts' lust: and they walked in their own counsels."* They followed their own way and their own counsel. Verse 13, *"Oh that my people had hearkened unto me, and Israel had walked in my ways!"* This is the heart of the King that we would listen to His voice and walk in His way.

As a princess to the King, your time in prayer should allow for time to listen to God as he speaks. He can speak through His word or through prayer. Psalms 46:10 says to, *"be still, and know that I am God:"* Pray is two-way conversation with the King. A princess should remember to do more listening than talking. If you are always talking, you are not listening.

Practice listening to God today.

Sunday:

Respect the Commandments of the King

In preparation for a day of worship, ask God to show you areas of your life that need to be changed, submitted to God, and how to encourage others within the fellowship of believers.

Psalms 119:5-8, *"O that my ways were directed to keep thy statutes! 6 Then shall I not be ashamed, when I have respect unto all thy commandments. 7 I will praise thee with uprightness of heart, when I shall have learned thy righteous judgments. 8 I will keep thy statutes: O forsake me not utterly."*

Help me to learn about you today that I might respect and keep your commandments. Open my heart to learn of areas in my life that I need to submit and forsake. Help me to praise You through an upright heart.

What did God show me today?

_____

_____

_____

_____

_____

What areas of my life do I need to submit to God?

_____

_____

_____

_____

_____

How can I be a blessing to others or encourage other believers today?

_____

_____

_____

_____

_____

How can I be a blessing to others or encourage others this week?

_____

_____

_____

_____

Privileges of a Princess

Monday:

Access to the Throne

According to the "The Seven Great Monarchies of the Eastern World, Or, The History, Geography and Antiquities of Chaldaea, Assyria, Babylon, Media, Persia, Parthia, and Sassanian Or New Persian Empire" (Rawlinson, 1885 p.351)

"…from the time of Darius I., there seem to have been seven great families, …, whose chiefs had the privilege of free communication with the monarch, and from which he was legally bound to choose his legitimate wives. The chiefs appear to have been known as "the Seven Princes," or "the Seven Counsellors of the king." They sat next to him as they recommended important measures of state, and were, in part, responsible for them public festivals; "'…they could demand admission to the monarch's presence at any time, unless he were in the female apartments; …. Excepting the "Seven Princes," no one could approach the royal person unless introduced by a Court usher.'" Prostration—the attitude of worship—was required of all as they entered the presence. "The hands of the persons introduced had to be hidden in their sleeves so long as their audience lasted." In crossing the Palace Courts it was necessary to abstain carefully from touching the carpet which was laid for the king to walk on. Coming into the king's presence unsummoned was a capital crime, punished by the attendants with instant death, unless the monarch himself, as a sign that he pardoned the intrusion, held out towards the culprit the golden sceptre which he bore in his hands. It was also a capital offence to sit down, even unknowingly, upon the royal throne;"'

Approaching the throne of the King was serious business. As a Christian, how are we to approach God's throne?

Read Ephesians 2:11-21.

Before we were saved, we did not have citizenship in Heaven. Through the finished work of Christ, we are brought near to God to have access or an audience with the King of Kings.

Romans 5:1-2 says that, *"Therefore being justified by faith, we have peace with God through our Lord Jesus Christ: 2 By whom also we have **access by faith** into this grace wherein we stand, and rejoice in hope of the glory of God."* [Emphasis added] We have access by faith in Christ Jesus.

As a daughter of the King, do you access the throne of the King? How often are you in His presence?

_____

_____

What is keeping you from the presence of the King of Kings?

_____

_____

_____

Isaiah 59:2, *"But your iniquities have separated between you and your God, and your sins have hid his face from you, that he will not hear."*

Isaiah realized that our iniquities (or sin) that separates us from God, just as Adam and Eve hid from God's presence in the Garden of Eden. What in your life is separating you from the presence of the King?

_____

_____

_____

_____

_____

Is it an over-committed schedule, a lack of want to on your part, or unconfessed sin? A princess should want to be in the presence of the king. A lack of desire should be a red flag in your Christian life. Ask God to show you what needs to change and to strengthen your walk.

Boldly Approaching the Throne

As a princess, you have access to the throne like the "Seven Princes" from King Darius' time. Take some time to read Ephesian 3:8-21. What verses stand out to you?

_____

_____

What was Paul saying?

Vs 8-10. Paul recognized in humility the grace that he had received through Christ. Through Christ you have unsearchable (incomprehensible) riches through all God has created and wisdom. Verse 11 shares that these riches are according to the eternal purpose.

Verse 12 tells us that through our relationship with Christ we can have boldness and access to the throne with confidence. We cannot overlook *"by the faith in him."* Faith and confidence in your God, His power, and authority gives you hope in the trials and tribulations that you face during your reign.

Paul then offered a prayer for the Ephesians to live a Christ honoring life.

*"14 For this cause **I bow my knees** unto the Father of our Lord Jesus Christ, 15 Of whom the whole family in heaven and earth is named, 16 That he would grant you, **according to the riches of his glory**, to be **strengthened** with might by his Spirit in the inner man; 17 That **Christ may dwell in your hearts by faith**; that ye, being **rooted** (a plant rooted cannot be easily pulled out of the ground) **and grounded in love**, 18 May be able to **comprehend** (understand) with all saints what is the breadth, and length, and depth, and height; 19 And to **know the love of Christ**, which passeth knowledge, that ye **might be filled** with*

41

all the fulness of God." [Emphasis and comments added] Christ has the power to go above all that we ask or think. So why would we not access the King of Kings, if we believe that he is all powerful?

James 4:2-3 tells us that, *"…yet ye have not, because ye ask not. 3 Ye ask, and receive not, because ye ask amiss* (badly), *that ye may consume it upon your lusts."*

Hebrews 10:18-21 says, *"Now where remission of these is, there is no more offering for sin. 19 Having therefore, brethren,* **boldness to enter into the holiest by the blood of Jesus**, *20 By a new and living way, which he hath consecrated for us, through the veil, that is to say, his flesh; 21 And having an high priest over the house of God;"* [Emphasis added] When Christ died on the cross the veil was torn between the inner temple and the holy of holies, this gave us boldness to enter into the court of the King of Kings.

Hebrews 4:14-16, *"Seeing then that we have a great high priest, that is passed into the heavens, Jesus the Son of God, let us hold fast our profession. 15 For we have not an high priest which cannot be touched with the feeling of our infirmities; but was in all points tempted like as we are, yet without sin. 16* **Let us therefore come boldly unto the throne of grace**, *that we may obtain mercy, and find grace to help in time of need.* [Emphasis added] Jesus Christ is our great high priest with verse 15 telling us that he is touched by our infirmities. The definition of infirmities from the *Strong's Concordance* is "want of strength, weakness, illness, suffering, calamity, and frailty." Paraphrasing verse 16 tells us to come boldly to the throne. Because you can ask the King of Kings about your needs, what are you praying for today? Does this include others? Does this include praying for others to be promoted to a princess and enjoy the same privileges that you have to the King?

Wednesday:

Power of the King

Revelation 19:1, *"And after these things I heard a great voice of much people in heaven, saying, Alleluia; Salvation, and glory, and honour, and power, unto the Lord our God:"*

Ephesian 1:17-23, *"That the God of our Lord Jesus Christ, the Father of glory, may give unto you the spirit of **wisdom and revelation in the knowledge of him**: 18 The **eyes of your understanding being enlightened**; that ye may know what is the hope of his calling, and what the riches of the glory of his inheritance in the saints, 19 And what is the **exceeding greatness of his power to us-ward who believe**, according to **the working of his mighty power**, 20 Which he wrought in Christ, when he raised him from the dead, and set him at his own right hand in the heavenly places, 21 **Far above all principality**, and **power, and might, and dominion, and every name that is named**, not only in this world, but also in that which is to come: 22 And hath put all things under his feet, and gave him to be the head over all things to the church, 23 Which is his body, the fulness of him that filleth all in all."* [Emphasis added] WOW!! God is all powerful, all knowing, all present. What a great truth that He is King overall and above everything of this world and beyond! God is the most powerful King. Do we approach Him as such? Are we reverent in His presence and respectful? As Christians, we have the privilege of calling him Abba Father. According to Bible Word Help, Abba Father means "used as the term of *tender endearment* by a beloved child – i.e. in an *affectionate, dependent* relationship with their father; '*daddy,*' '*papa.*'" We have direct access to God through Christ and the Holy Spirit. Philippians 4:13 tells us, *"we can do all things through Christ who strengths us"* [paraphrased from KJV].

2 Peter 1:3-4 goes on to say, *"According as his **divine power** hath given unto us all things that pertain **unto life and godliness,** through the knowledge of him that hath called us to glory and virtue: 4 Whereby are given unto us exceeding great and precious promises: that by these ye might be partakers of the divine nature, having escaped the corruption that is in the world through lust"* [Emphasis added] Then 2 Timothy 3:5, warns that, *"Having a form of godliness, but denying the power thereof: from such turn away."*

Do you know that God is all powerful? Do you live like He is all powerful?

Do you heed His Word, because of His power and might? Are you serious about the King of Kings?

Thursday:

Authority of the King

Read Colossians 1:9-20.

What does it say?

As a Princess to the King of Kings, you need to desperately understand His authority over your life. Verse 16 tells us that *"all things created, that are in heaven, and that are in earth, visible and invisible, whether they be thrones, or dominions, or principalities, or powers: all things were created by him, and for him:"* What a mighty God we serve!

In Luke 9:1-2, *"Then he called his twelve disciples together, and gave them **power and authority over all** devils, and to cure diseases. 2 And he sent them to preach the kingdom of God, and to heal the sick"* [Emphasis added] Jesus, as the Son of God, gave His disciples power and authority. Only someone with authority can delegate or give it to someone else. Jesus gave them power to perform miracles, so they could give God the glory and share the gospel (the good news of Christ's death, burial, and resurrection for our sins).

Mark 4:39-41, *"And he arose, and rebuked the wind, and said unto the sea, Peace, be still. And the wind ceased, and there was a great calm. 40 And he said unto them, Why are ye so fearful? how is it that ye have no faith? 41 And they feared exceedingly, and said one to another, **What manner of man is this, that even the wind and the sea obey him?"*** [Emphasis added] Jesus showed His authority over elements of the world.

Have you given the King authority over your heart and life?

Are there areas of your life you are holding back? Ask God to search your heart and open the closets of your heart and mind that He wants to clean out?

What will it take for you to obey the authority of God?

_____

_____

_____

_____

_____

Friday:

Wisdom from the King

Read 1 Kings 4:29-34.

Solomon's wisdom was given by God. He was wise and attracted other kings to himself. The King can give you wisdom.

James 1:5-6 says, *"If any of you **lack wisdom**, let him **ask of God**, that giveth to all men liberally, and upbraideth not; and it shall be given him. 6 But let him **ask in faith, nothing wavering**. For he that wavereth is like a wave of the sea driven with the wind and tossed."* [Emphasis added]

Why do we need wisdom and discernment?

What are they?

_____

_____

_____

The "why" is provided in Proverbs 4:7-9 which states, *"Wisdom is the principal thing; therefore get wisdom: and with all thy getting get understanding. 8 Exalt her, and she shall promote thee: she shall bring thee to honour, when thou dost embrace her. 9 She shall give to thine head an ornament of grace: a crown of glory shall she deliver to thee."*

According to *Strong's Concordance*, wisdom is "skillful, wisely, wit" while discernment is to "understand."

Proverbs 4 tells us that both wisdom and discernment are both important. Psalms 119:125 states that, *"I am thy servant; give me understanding, that I may know thy testimonies."* Wisdom and discernment are needed by a princess to identify false ways as indicated further in Psalms 119:128, *"Therefore I esteem all thy precepts concerning* *all things to be right; and **I hate every false way**.*" How can you hate false ways if you do not have wisdom or discernment? [Emphasis added]

_____

_____

Pray today that God will give you both wisdom and discernment as you learn to be a Princess to the Throne of Grace.

Saturday:

Living in the Palace
In my house you follow my rules

Have your parents ever told you, "as long as you live in my house you will follow my rules?" If not, have you heard others in authority over you expecting you to obey the rules? As a Princess to the Throne, our loving and kind God expects our obedience (following His laws) out of love for Him. 1 John 5:3 says, *"For this is the love of God, that we keep His commandments: and His commandments are not grievous."*

Read John 15:1-12.

What does "abide" mean?

_____

_____

_____

What important lesson is Jesus teaching in this passage?

_____

_____

_____

_____

_____

Abide, according to *Strong's Concordance* is to "continue, dwell, *and* remain." It is "a primary verb; to stay (in a given place, state, relation or expectancy) -- abide, continue, dwell, endure, be present, remain, stand, tarry (for), X thine own." Jesus is teaching us the importance of our dependency on the Almighty God. Just as the branch cannot survive without the direct source of nourishment and support provided by the vine, neither can a princess survive the expectations set forth by her position without the strength and support of the King. As we continually dwell or remove our own way from the picture, we become dependent on Jesus Christ and God to direct our paths. The commandments that are put in front of us in God's word are precious, meaningful and followed out of love for the King. As 1 John 5:3 shares, when we follow God's commandments out of love that they are not "grievous" or "heavy, weighty, or burdensome (*Strong's Concordance*)."

Princess, how are you abiding in Christ?

_____

_____

_____

_____

_____

Sunday:

Hearken to the King

In preparation for a day of worship, ask God to show you areas of your life that need to be changed, submitted to God, and how to encourage others within the fellowship of believers.

Jeremiah 29:12-13, *"Then shall ye call upon me, and ye shall go and pray unto me, and I will hearken unto you. 13 And ye shall seek me, and find me, when ye shall search for me with all your heart."*

Pray that God would open your eyes today as we seek to know God and His will for our lives.

What did God show me today?

_____
_____
_____
_____
_____

What areas of my life do I need to submit to God?

_____
_____
_____
_____
_____

How can I be a blessing to others or encourage other believers today?

_____
_____
_____
_____

How can I be a blessing to others or encourage others this week?

_____

_____

_____

_____

_____

Royal Duties as a Princess

A princess is always in the spot light in her kingdom. The King has provided some guidelines to follow for His princess. As a Princess to the Throne of Grace, you have royal duties that guide your actions.

Loving the King Above All Others

Read Matthew 22:34-40.

What did Jesus say about the greatest commandment?

_____

_____

_____

Jesus told the Pharisees that, *"Thou shalt love the Lord thy God with all thy heart, and with all thy soul, and with all thy mind. This is the first and great commandment."* What does this mean for a daughter of the King of Kings?

How do you love God with all your heart, soul and mind?

_____

_____

_____

_____

_____

53

God wants your full focus and attention. According to the *Strong's Concordance*, the heart refers to your inner life or your intention. *HELPS Word Study* provides additional insight as "our "desire-*decisions*" that establish who we really are." For the soul, *Strong's Concordance* states "the soul as the seat of affections and will." For the mind, *Strong's Concordance* shares that this is "understanding, intellect, mind, [and] insight." So if God wants you to love Him with your intentions, your desires, your understanding, intellect, and insight.

When we do not surrender our will to the King, we are breaking the most important law in the Kingdom. God said to the Israelites if they loved Him they would keep His commandments. Exodus 20:7-10 also reminds us that God is a jealous God not wanting us to put other gods before Him. Our graven images in today's world can be more subtle than a golden calf we worship. Idols may come in different forms. Meriam Webster states that an idol is one that is greatly admired or an image of something worshipped. Do you get as upset about losing your Bible as misplacing your phone? Do you spend more time thinking about movies than God?

What do you put before God?

_____

_____

_____

_____

_____

Have you examined your intentions and the decisions you make?

I John 5:20-21 warns that we should stay away from idols. *"And we know that the Son of God is come, and hath given us an understanding, that we may know him that is true, and we are in him that is true, even in His Son Jesus Christ. This is the true God, and eternal life. 21 Little children, keep yourselves from idols. Amen.*" Take some time to reflect on your life. Do you love the King of Kings with all your heart, soul, and mind?

Tuesday:

Praising the King

Read Psalm 150.

As a daughter of the King, do you praise Him? Are your lips filled with the praise of His excellent greatness? Do you have a song in your heart that praises the King? Psalms 150:6 says, *"Let every thing that hath breath praise the LORD. Praise ye the LORD."*

Psalms 63:1-7 states, *"O God, **thou art my** God; **early will I seek thee**: my **soul thirsteth** [the desire from Monday] for thee, my flesh **longeth** for thee in a dry and thirsty land, where no water is; 2 To see thy power and thy glory, so as I have seen thee in the sanctuary. 3 Because thy lovingkindness is better than life, **my lips shall praise thee**. 4 Thus will I bless thee while I live: I will lift up my hands in thy name. 5 My soul shall be satisfied as with marrow and fatness; and my mouth shall praise thee with **joyful lips**: 6 When I remember thee upon my bed, and **meditate** on thee in the night watches. 7 Because thou hast been my help, therefore in the shadow of thy wings will **I rejoice**."* [Emphasis added] The Psalmists was going to praise God because of who he was and had recognized the lovingkindness God had given that justifies praising the King.

Does your soul desire the things of God?

Are you quick to give God praise in all situations?

Do you long to praise Him and meditate on His lovingkindness?

Write down a praise list. No matter what your circumstances, you can always praise Him.

- My Salvation
- You are all knowing

- You are all powerful
-
-
-
-
-
-

Hebrews 13:15, "*By him therefore let us offer the sacrifice of praise to God continually, that is, the fruit of our lips giving thanks to His name.*"

Wednesday:

Sacrificing for the King

Being in the spotlight is not easy. It requires sacrificing your wants in exchange for the abundance of protection and the joy of pleasing the King, as well as advancing the Kingdom.

What is a sacrifice?

According to Meriam-Webster, a sacrifice is "an act of offering to a deity something precious."

Read Hebrews 13:5-17.

What do the verses say about your conversation?

_____

_____

_____

What does content mean?

_____

_____

Does Jesus Christ change?

_____

_____

How often are we to offer sacrifice?

_____

_____

When we submit to those in authority over us, how should we respond?

_____

_____

As daughters of the King, we must learn the art of sacrificing for and to the King. We were told in Hebrews to not be jealous or envious of others, to be satisfied with what we have, and to obey with joy.

Does your face reflect the characteristics above when sacrificing is required? Do we walk around with pouty faces when we do not get what we want? Do we murmur and complain with the high standards required by the King of Kings to live pure lives?

Romans 12:1, *"I beseech you therefore, brethren, by the mercies of God, that ye present your bodies a **living sacrifice**, holy, acceptable unto God, which is your reasonable service."* [Emphasis added] God views the sacrifices that we have to make to advance the Kingdom as our reasonable service for being a daughter of the King.

What are some struggles you have with being a living sacrifice?

_____

_____

_____

_____

_____

Thursday:

Sharing the King

Matthew 9:35-38, *"And Jesus went about all the cities and villages, teaching in their synagogues, and preaching the gospel of the kingdom, and healing every sickness and every disease among the people. 36 But when he saw the multitudes, he was moved with compassion on them, because they fainted, and were scattered abroad, as sheep having no shepherd. 37 Then saith he unto his disciples, The harvest truly is plenteous, but the labourers are few; 38 Pray ye therefore the Lord of the harvest, that he will send forth labourers into his harvest."*

Jesus was our earthly example. He was sharing the King with others throughout His time on this Earth. Jesus shared the love of God with others throughout His ministry. The disciples then continued preaching the good news or the gospel to see others come to know Christ. Read Acts 2:38-47.

Are you sharing the King with others?

Do you believe the word of God is true? Do you believe the words of Jesus that He is the only way to be a daughter of the King of Kings?

Paul wrote in Romans 1:16, *"For I am not ashamed of the gospel of Christ: for it is the power of God unto salvation to every one that believeth; to the Jew first, and also to the Greek."* Do you believe the King of Kings will change peoples' lives? Do you believe He will give them hope and adopted them into His family? Do you believe they can go from forever separated from God to calling Him Abba Father?

Pray that God will give you someone to share the King with this week. Who do you need to tell?

Loving those in the Kingdom

John 13:34-35, *"A new commandment I give unto you, That ye love one another; as I have **loved** you, that ye also **love** one another. 35 By this shall all men know that ye are my disciples, if ye have **love** one to another."* [Emphasis added]

As a princess, you should love those in the kingdom. John 13:34 states *"as I have loved you."* What do you think that means?

_____

_____

_____

How does God love us? How does He show love to us?

_____

_____

_____

_____

_____

Read 1 John 4:7-21.

I love how the passage starts. "Beloved" in *Strong's Concordance* defines this as "loved, beloved, with two special applications: the Beloved, a title of the Messiah (Christ), as beloved beyond all others by the God who sent Him; of Christians, as beloved by God, Christ, and one another." As you reflect on this passage, why should we love one another?

_____

_____

_____

What does it show if we love one another?

_____

_____

_____

Verse 11 and 12 state, *"Beloved, if God so loved us, we ought also to love one another. 12 No man hath seen God at any time. If we love one another, God dwelleth in us, and his love is perfected in us."* Then verse 13 lets us know that we have His Spirit. Verse 20 has some strong language about hating others and saying that we love God. Are you quick to love?

Are you fearful to love as in verse 18?

Do you have strong feelings of hate toward others?

_____

_____

Romans 14:13, *"Let us not therefore judge one another any more: but judge this rather, that no man put a stumblingblock or an occasion to fall in his brother's way."*

Luke 6:27-38 says, *"But I say unto you which hear,* **Love your enemies**, *do* **good to them which hate you**, *28 Bless them that curse you, and pray for them which* **despitefully use you**. *29 And unto him that smiteth thee on the one cheek* **offer also the other**; *and him that taketh away thy cloke forbid not to take thy coat also. 30 Give to every man that asketh of thee; and of him that taketh away thy goods ask them not again. 31 And as ye would that men should do to you, do ye also to them likewise. 32 For if ye love them which love you, what thank have ye? for sinners also love those that love them. 33 And if ye do good to them which do good to you,* **what thank have ye?** *for sinners also do even the same. 34 And if ye lend to them of whom ye hope to receive, what thank have ye? for sinners also lend to sinners, to receive as much again. 35 But* *love ye your enemies, and do good, and lend, hoping for nothing again*; *and your reward shall be great, and ye shall be the children of the Highest: for he is **kind unto the unthankful** and to the evil. 36 Be ye therefore **merciful**, as your Father also is merciful. 37 **Judge not**, and ye shall not be judged: **condemn not**, and ye shall not be condemned: **forgive, and ye shall be forgiven:** 38 Give, and it shall be given unto you; good measure, pressed down, and shaken together, and running over, shall men give into your bosom. For with the same measure that ye mete withal it shall be **measured to you again**."* [Emphasis added]

As a princess, you should be forgiving, merciful, doing good to those who treat you badly, and lend hope to others. In verse 33 and 34, the Bible says *"what thank have ye?"* What does this mean?

_____

_____

_____

This passage is telling us that sinners can love those that love them and give hope to those to receive. As *"children of the Highest,"* we are called to be kind to those who are unthankful, turn the other cheek, give more than what they take, forgive them as we have been forgiven, and show mercy.

1 Peter 1:22, *"Seeing ye have purified your souls in obeying the truth through the Spirit unto unfeigned love of the brethren, **see that ye love one another with a pure heart fervently**: 23 Being born again, not of corruptible seed, but of incorruptible, by the word of God, which liveth and abideth for ever."* [Emphasis added]

Do you love others with a pure heart? Do you love them fervently?

Saturday:

Serving in the Kingdom

As a Princess to the Throne, your service is required in the kingdom. Luke 4:8, *"And Jesus answered and said unto him, Get thee behind me, Satan: for it is written, Thou shalt worship the Lord thy God, and him only shalt thou serve."* Jesus told Satan that we are to worship and serve only God.

Colossians 3:22-25 says, *"Servants, obey in all things your masters according to the flesh; not with* **eyeservice***, as menpleasers; but in singleness of heart, fearing God: 23 And whatsoever ye do,* **do it heartily***, as to the Lord, and not unto men; 24 Knowing that of the Lord ye shall receive the reward of the inheritance: for ye serve the Lord Christ. 25 But he that doeth wrong shall receive for the wrong which he hath done: and there is no respect of persons."* [Emphasis added]

The King of Kings is asking us to obey with the right intentions. What does *"Not with eyeservice"* mean? What do we do when no one is watching? Do we continue to do things *"heartily"* when no one is watching?

Read Philippians 2:5-18.

Verse 12-13 Paul writes, *"Wherefore, my beloved, as ye have always obeyed, not as in my presence only, but now much more in my absence, work out your own salvation with fear and trembling. 13 For it is God which worketh in you both to will and to do of his good pleasure."*

He goes on to tell us that we need to, *"Do all things without murmurings and disputings: 15 That ye may be blameless and harmless, ..."* Paul wanted to know that he had not run the race in vain and he wants us to experience the same.

Do you do all things without murmuring or disputing? Are you quick to argue?

What struggles do you have in serving in the Kingdom?

_____

_____

_____

_____

_____

How can God strengthen you for service in the Kingdom? What do you need to give to Him?

_____

_____

_____

_____

_____

Philippians 4:13-14, *"I can do all things through Christ which strengtheneth me. 14 Notwithstanding ye have well done, that ye did communicate with my affliction."*

Sunday:

Worshipping the King

In preparation for a day of worship, ask God to show you areas of your life that need to be changed, submitted to God, and how to encourage others within the fellowship of believers.

Pray this scripture.

Psalms 51:4-12, *"Against thee, thee only, have I sinned, and done this evil in thy sight: that thou mightest be justified when thou speakest, and be clear when thou judgest. 5 Behold, I was shapen in iniquity; and in sin did my mother conceive me. 6 Behold, thou desirest truth in the inward parts: and in the hidden part thou shalt make me to know wisdom. 7 Purge me with hyssop, and I shall be clean: wash me, and I shall be whiter than snow. 8 Make me to hear joy and gladness; that the bones which thou hast broken may rejoice. 9 Hide thy face from my sins, and blot out all mine iniquities. 10 Create in me a clean heart, O God; and renew a right spirit within me. 11 Cast me not away from thy presence; and take not thy holy spirit from me. 12 Restore unto me the joy of thy salvation; and uphold me with thy free spirit.*

What did God show me today?

_____

_____

_____

_____

_____

What areas of my life do I need to submit to God?

_____

_____

_____

_____

_____

How can I be a blessing to others or encourage other believers today?

_____

_____

_____

_____

How can I be a blessing to others or encourage others this week?

_____

_____

_____

_____

Dressing Like a Princess

As a child of the King, imagine in your mind how you look as a princess. Take a minute or two to sketch the key components of your imagine or find a picture of how you look as a princess.

As many of us imagine ourselves as a princess, we may have a large ball gown with a beautiful tiara. We will notice our hair, shoes, jewelry, and many other small details as we put together the picture in our mind. Maybe it is hard for you to imagine yourself as a princess because of hurtful words by others. The King of Kings loves His daughters with a perfect love. God wants what is best for each of us, but we have to put our trust in Him. We have to be ready for His direction in our lives with a "No, that is not the best for you right now," or "I need you to take care of this in your life, so I can give you the desires of your heart," or "Yes, this is my perfect will for your life." Are you ready to make this commitment as a daughter of the King?

Monday:

Princess Attire

What are some key components in your image that the King of Kings is interested in for His princess?

_____

_____

_____

_____

_____

Read Ephesians 6:11-17.

As a Princess to the Throne of Grace, what are the key elements you should have in your royal closet? Why are these things important?

_____

_____

_____

_____

_____

As a child of the King, we are in battle against the Prince of Darkness. He is trying to rule over our life and take control of the throne. As a princess to the King of Kings, part of our royal attire has to include battle gear. Even as a Princess, we enter into battle daily fighting our own desires of what we want and what feels good, as well as fighting against fiery darts that are hurled at us by the devil. Each day we make choices to do right. Doing what we want or going against the King's orders are both easier for us than following the commands set forth by the King.

1 Corinthians 10:10-13 tells us, *"Neither murmur ye, as some of them also murmured, and were destroyed of the destroyer. 11 Now all these things happened unto them for ensamples: and they are written for our admonition,*

*upon whom the ends of the world are come. 12 **Wherefore let him that thinketh he standeth take heed lest he fall.** 13 There hath no temptation taken you but such as is common to man: but God is faithful, who will not suffer you to be tempted above that ye are able; but will with the temptation also make a way to escape, that ye may be able to bear it."* [Emphasis added]

Take heed Princess!!

1 Peter 5:6-8, *"Humble yourselves therefore under the mighty hand of God, that he may exalt you in due time: 7 Casting all your care upon him; for he careth for you. 8 Be sober, be vigilant; because your adversary the devil, as a roaring lion, walketh about, seeking whom he may devour:"*

Do you have your princess attire? Is your heart, head, and mind protected against the devil through your armor? What areas does the King want to improve in your life?

_____

_____

_____

_____

_____

Tuesday:

Public Appearances

As a daughter of the King of Kings, you are on stage inside your home and outside your home. People are watching you to see how you are going to act and react out in various situations. Proverbs 16:31-33, *"The hoary head* **[old age]** *is a* **crown of glory**, *if it be found in* **the way of righteousness**. *32 He that is* **slow to anger** *is better than the mighty; and* **he that ruleth his spirit** *than he that taketh a city. 33 The lot is cast into the lap; but the whole disposing thereof is of the LORD."* [Emphasis added] Some of our wisdom comes from learning through experiences, hence the crown of glory through old age. The Bible tells us that the path is found in righteousness. The kingdom increases in strength and might when we are slow to anger and rule our spirit. Is it tough for you to be slow to anger? Is it a challenge to rule over your spirit? You may even ask what that means. The *Strong's Concordance* defines this as "he that ruleth" as having command over and "his spirit" as breath or wind. Through the help of the King's training for us (His Word) and through polishing school (church, wise counsel, parents, prayer and study of the King's wishes), a princess is ready to meet the public. As a princess, we cannot lose control out and about.

Proverbs 22:1-4, *"***A good name*** is rather to be chosen than great riches, and* **loving favour** *rather than silver and gold. 2 The rich and poor meet together: the LORD is the maker of them all. 3* **A prudent man** *foreseeth the evil, and hideth himself: but the simple pass on, and are punished. 4* **By humility and the fear of the LORD** *are riches, and honour, and life."* [Emphasis added] To many affluent families, your name and reputation is important. The King of Kings is telling you that your "good name" or your reputation and "loving favour" or kindness and grace are more important than riches of this world.

Do not compromise these when you are out. *"A prudent man"* or sensible man hides from evil with humility or "freedom from pride or arrogance" (Merriam-Webster Dictionary) and with fear of the Lord. The King knows the choices you make.

Proverbs 14:28, 34-35, *"In the multitude of people is the **king's honour**: but in the **want of people** is the destruction of the prince... 34 **Righteousness** exalteth a nation: but sin is a reproach to any people. 35 **The king's favour is toward a wise servant**: but his wrath is against him that causeth shame."* [Emphasis added] The King is honored by your actions. Be a wise daughter.

Proverbs 13:1-12, *"A wise son **heareth his father's instruction**: but a scorner heareth not rebuke. 2 A man shall eat good by the fruit of his mouth: but the soul of the transgressors shall eat violence. 3 He that keepeth his mouth keepeth his life: but he that openeth wide his lips shall have destruction. 4 The soul of the sluggard desireth, and hath nothing: but the soul of the diligent shall be made fat. 5 A righteous man hateth lying: but a wicked man is loathsome, and cometh to shame. 6 Righteousness keepeth him that is upright in the way: but wickedness overthroweth the sinner. 7 There is that maketh himself rich, yet hath nothing: there is that maketh himself poor, yet hath great riches. 8 The ransom of a man's life are his riches: but the poor heareth not rebuke. 9 The light of the righteous rejoiceth: but the lamp of the wicked shall be put out. 10 Only by pride cometh contention: but with the well advised is wisdom. 11 Wealth gotten by vanity shall be diminished: but he that gathereth by labour shall increase. 12 Hope deferred maketh the heart sick: but when the desire cometh, it is a tree of life."* [Emphasis added] As a daughter of the King, you should be listening to the Father's instructions on how to act in public.

What are some key words in Proverbs 13?

_____

_____

_____

_____

_____

What is God speaking to you about?

_____

_____

_____

_____

As you look at this, you are given some things to do and not to do.

1) Do not tell everything you know (verse 3).

2) Do not be lazy, but be diligent (Verse 4).

3) Do not lie (Verse 5).

4) Do not be around the wicked as they will bring you down with them (Verse 6). This includes your choice of friends.

5) Riches and wealth do not satisfy your need for the King of Kings (Verse 7 and 8), as well as be careful not to chase riches. God will bless in His timing.

6) Leading a righteous life brings happiness instead of guilt. (Verse 9)

7) Be careful of pride and thinking highly of yourself (Verse 10)

8) If you work hard for something it will mean more (Vere 11)

Read 1 Thessalonians 5:8-24.

In 1 Thessalonians 5:8-24 what guidance is given to the daughter of the King?

_____

_____

_____

_____

As you read these verses, God's word provides standards for your actions. Be sober (calm), because through Christ we have battle gear (faith, hope, love and grace). Provide comfort to others and build others up (edify). Warn them that are going down the wrong path or those that worry. Be patient and do not repay evil for evil, but show grace to all. Rejoice and pray always. As a daughter of the King, you have many responsibilities and God has high expectations for your public appearances.

Wednesday:

The King's Standards

2 Corinthians 6:16-18, *"And what agreement hath the temple of God with idols? for* **ye are the temple of the living God***; as God hath said, I will dwell in them, and walk in them; and I will be their God, and they shall be my people. 17 Wherefore come out from among them, and* **be ye separate***, saith the Lord, and touch not the unclean thing; and I will receive you, 18 And will be a Father unto you, and ye* **shall be** *my sons and* **daughters***, saith the Lord Almighty."* [Emphasis added] The King of Kings calls His daughters to be separated and that your bodies are the temple of the living God.

> According to "The Seven Great Monarchies of the Eastern World, Or, The History, Geography and Antiquities of Chaldaea, Assyria, Babylon, Media, Persia, Parthia, and Sassanian Or New Persian Empire" (Rawlinson, 1885 p.351)

> Excepting the "Seven Princes," no one could approach the royal person unless introduced by a court usher. "'Prostration—the attitude of worship—was required of all as they entered the presence." The hands of the persons introduced had to be hidden in their sleeves so long as their audience lasted. "'In crossing the Palace Courts it was necessary to abstain carefully from touching the carpet which was laid for the king to walk on. "… and it was a grave misdemeanor to wear one of the king's cast-off dresses.'" Etiquette was almost as severe on the monarch himself as on his subjects. He was required to live chiefly in seclusion;'" to eat his meals, for the most part, alone; "'never to go on foot beyond the palace walls;'"

Again as daughters of the King, you are called to be separate. Does this mean you cannot have friends and live alone? No, but it does mean that as a daughter of the King you should not be involved in things that displease the King. As with public appearances, the expectations are high.

Read Proverbs 19:1-19.

What are these verses saying?

_____

_____

_____

_____

_____

The King's standards include having integrity; being knowledgeable, honest, trustworthy, giving and discerning, being slow to anger; and choosing friends carefully. Here are some other standards set forth by the King.

The King gives us a royal law in James 2:8-10, *"If ye fulfil the royal law according to the scripture, Thou shalt **love thy neighbour as thyself**, ye do well: 9 But if ye have **respect to persons**, ye commit sin, and are convinced of the law as transgressors. 10 For whosoever shall keep the whole law, and yet offend in one point, he is guilty of all."* Do you love people as you do yourself? Do you treat clean, well-dressed people differently than the poor?" [Emphasis added]

God also warns in many places about our speech and our tongue. Matt 12:32-37 says, *"And whosoever speaketh a word against the Son of man, it shall be forgiven him: but whosoever speaketh against the Holy Ghost, it shall not be forgiven him, neither in this world, neither in the world to come. 33 Either make the tree good, and his fruit good; or else make the tree corrupt, and his fruit corrupt: for the tree is known by his* *fruit. 34 O generation of vipers, how can ye, being evil, speak good things? for **out of the abundance of the heart the mouth speaketh**. 35 A good man out of the good treasure of the heart bringeth forth good things: and an evil man out of the evil treasure bringeth forth evil things. 36 But I say unto you, **That every idle word that men shall speak**, they shall give account thereof in the day of judgment. 37 For by thy words thou shalt be justified, and by thy words thou shalt be condemned.* " [Emphasis added] What is in your heart will come out of your mouth? You will give an account for every word that comes out of your mouth. Is it pleasing to the King? God tells us not to use His name or Jesus's name in dishonor. Be careful about abbreviations that the world uses to dishonor the King and slang word for this such as "Gosh."

Which King's standards do you struggle with?

_____

_____

_____

_____

_____

Thursday:

Setting an Example

As daughters of the King, God has called us to be examples to others. We should not be comparing ourselves with those around us, but to the standards and commands set forth by the King. 1 Peter 3:3-5, *"Neither as being lords over God's heritage, but **being ensamples** to the flock. 4 And when the **chief Shepherd** [Christ] shall appear, ye shall receive a crown of glory that fadeth not away. 5 Likewise, ye younger, **submit yourselves** unto the elder. Yea, all of you be subject one to another, and **be clothed with humility**: for God resisteth the proud, and giveth grace to the **humble**."* [Emphasis added]

Read Matthew 5:13-6:25.

Write down what Jesus was asking the daughters of the King of Kings to do in these verses.

_____

_____

_____

_____

_____

As you read through this, Christ speaks in Matthew 5:13 to being salt of the earth, in 16 being a light to others, in 22 the dangers of anger, in 27-30 how to handle temptation, in 39-40 the importance of forgiveness, in 44 loving your enemies, in 6:1 giving with the right attitude, in 5 earnest prayer, in 16-18 our countenance in fasting, in 19 our reward in heaven, and in 25 why we should not worry. The Bible also gives examples of what we should follow to be a good example, as in 2 Timothy 2:22, *"Flee also youthful lusts: but follow righteousness, faith, charity, peace, with them that call on the Lord out of a pure heart."*

It is so easy to do what we want to do *"youthful lusts,"* but it is more difficult to be pure in heart and follow the commands of the King. 1 Peter 5:5-7 says, *"Likewise, ye younger,* **submit yourselves** *unto the elder. Yea, all of you be subject one to another, and be clothed with humility: for God resisteth the proud, and giveth grace to the humble. 6 Humble yourselves therefore under the mighty hand of God, that he may exalt you in due time: 7 Casting all your care upon him; for he careth for you."* [Emphasis added] Is it hard to submit to authorities? Do you find it difficult to submit to those with wisdom around you whether it be a parent, teacher, or pastor?

_____

_____

_____

_____

_____

How do you handle it when you are corrected by wise counsel?

_____

_____

_____

_____

Friday:

Latest Fashions

In our culture today, fashion, clothing, and brand names are bombarding us, as well as how we look. Matthew 6:28-34, *"And why take ye thought for raiment* [**clothing**]*? Consider the lilies of the field, how they grow; they toil not, neither do they spin: 29 And yet I say unto you, That even Solomon in all his glory was not arrayed like one of these. 30 Wherefore, if God so clothe the grass of the field, which today is, and tomorrow is cast into the oven, shall he not much more clothe you, O ye of little faith? 31 Therefore take no thought, saying, What shall we eat? or, What shall we drink? or, Wherewithal shall we be clothed? 32 (For after all these things do the Gentiles seek:) for your heavenly Father knoweth that ye have need of all these things. 33 But seek ye first the kingdom of God, and his righteousness; and all these things shall be added unto you. 34 Take therefore no thought for the morrow: for the morrow shall take thought for the things of itself. Sufficient unto the day is the evil thereof."* [Emphasis added]

Do you worry about what you are going to wear, how you are going to look and what you look like? Jesus warned us not to be overly concerned about our clothes or worry about the things we need. As a Princess to the King, God does not want us to be distracted by the things of this world. Does this mean we should not be neat, clean, and dressed nicely? As you look at *"clean"* in the Bible, God discussed the condition of you heart. He did tell us when we fast to *"wash thy face"* in Matthew 6:17. You will have trouble reaching out to others if you are dirty, smelly, and not dressed modestly. God wants to use you to reach others, so you will need to bathe, use deodorant, and dress pleasing to God to represent Him in the world.

Read Psalms 45:1-13.

What does the Psalmist say about the daughters of the King in this passage?

_____

_____

_____

The daughters of the King smelled good and were dressed in royal garments. God gave us an example of a woman in Proverbs 31 to live by in this world. She made sure her family and servants had coats for the snow. Proverbs 31:21-25 *"She is not afraid of the snow for her household: for all her household are clothed with scarlet. 22 She maketh herself coverings of tapestry; her clothing is silk and purple. 23 Her husband is known in the gates, when he sitteth among the elders of the land. 24 She maketh fine linen, and selleth it; and delivereth girdles unto the merchant. 25 Strength and honour are her clothing; and she shall rejoice in time to come."* They were clothed in scarlet, silk and purple, all of which were expensive fabrics. She was elegant, resourceful and full of strength, honor, and happiness. She took care of herself and her family. 1 Timothy 2:9, *"In like manner also, that women adorn themselves in **modest apparel**, with shamefacedness and sobriety; not with broided hair, or gold, or pearls, or costly array;"* [Emphasis added] You should be modest in your dress. What does this mean to you? The world we are in shows you low cut tops, short skirts, and tight fitting clothes. Think about what you are wearing. Would you feel comfortable in your outfit if Jesus was standing next to you? It is not about what everyone else is wearing. Is it pleasing to the King? What are your standards of modesty?

_____

_____

_____

Saturday:

Royal Garments

Isaiah 61:10-11, *"I will greatly rejoice in the LORD, my soul shall be joyful in my God; for he hath clothed me with the garments of salvation, he hath covered me with the robe of righteousness, as a bridegroom decketh himself with ornaments, and as a bride adorneth herself with her jewels. 11 For as the earth bringeth forth her bud, and as the garden causeth the things that are sown in it to spring forth; so the Lord GOD will cause righteousness and praise to spring forth before all the nations."* Isaiah 62:5, *"…and as the bridegroom rejoiceth over the bride, so shall thy God rejoice over thee."* As a daughter of the King, God wants you to be dressed in your royal garments. He wants you waiting and watching for His arrival as a bride waits for her husband for that special day. Revelation 21:2, *"And I John saw the holy city, new Jerusalem, coming down from God out of heaven, prepared as a bride adorned for her husband."* As a bride watching and waiting for her wedding day, she is busy making preparations, getting her dress ready, envisioning her special day. Jeremiah 2:32, *"Can a maid forget her ornaments, or a bride her attire? yet my people have forgotten me days without number."* A bride is not going to forget her dress or shoes or jewelry for her special day. She is going to triple check everything to make sure she is ready.

Read Esther 2:1-17.

Esther had to prepare for her one opportunity with the King and was purified for a year. She was bathed in oils and educated on the duties and expectations of being a queen. Because of her actions and her relationship with God, she found favor with the king's servants.

John 3:29-31, *"He that hath the bride is the bridegroom: but the friend of the bridegroom, which standeth and heareth him, rejoiceth greatly because of the bridegroom's voice: this my joy therefore is fulfilled. 30 He must increase, but I must decrease. 31 He that cometh from above is above all: he that is of the earth is earthly, and speaketh of the earth: he that cometh from heaven is above all."* John tells us that a bride is responding to the voice of the bridegroom. Do we respond to the voice of the bridegroom? Who is the bridegroom? Jesus is the bridegroom as a daughter of the King of Kings.

Are you prepared to meet the King? Are you clean in His sight?

_____

_____

_____

_____

_____

Sunday:

The King's Guidance

In preparation for a day of worship, ask God to show you areas of your life that need to be changed, submitted to God, and how to encourage others within the fellowship of believers.

Pray and ask God to show you great and mighty things. Pray that he will open your eyes to the things that need to change in your life and for the next steps in your life.

Jeremiah 33:3, *"Call unto me, and I will answer thee, and shew thee great and mighty things, which thou knowest not."*

What did God show me today?

_____

_____

_____

_____

_____

What areas of my life do I need to submit to God?

_____

_____

_____

_____

_____

How can I be a blessing to others or encourage other believers today?

_____

_____

_____

How can I be a blessing to others or encourage others this week?

_____

_____

_____

_____

_____

Walking Like a Princess

Have you ever seen a movie or show that has a royal family in it? If so, have you seen how the kingdom and even people from other counties treat the princess or the queen? That position of leadership and stature in the community causes other to share a sense of reverence and respect for that person. As a Princess to the Throne of Grace, God shares in His word the truths of walking like a princess.

Monday:

Stand up Straight

The Bible tells us in Psalms 138:14, *"I will praise thee; for I am fearfully and wonderfully made: marvellous are thy works; and that my soul knoweth right well."* As a Princess to the Throne of Grace, you are fearfully (cause astonishment and awe of God) and wonderfully (separate, set apart) made. God made you unique and special. We can bring all our doubt and fear about our position in the royal family to Him. He created you for a purpose to serve in the kingdom?

What are some of the unique and special gifts that God has given you?

_____

_____

_____

Maybe you could not think of anything; maybe you feel blessed by all God has given you; or maybe you have been hurt by others and find it difficult to see the good that God has created in you. God's response is for you Princess to stand up straight as a daughter to the King of Kings. 1 John 2:6 says *"He that saith he abideth in him ought himself also so to walk, even as he* (Jesus Christ) *walked."* [Clarification added]

Read Colossians 1.

Paul is writing a letter to the church in Colosse. He sees the fruit of the transformation that the gospel has made in their lives and shares about a faithful minister of the faith. Paul was praying that they would be *"filled with the knowledge of His* (God's) *will"* [Clarification added] applying it to their wisdom and they would have understanding for spiritual things.

Vs 10, *"That ye might **walk worthy of the Lord** unto all pleasing, being **fruitful in every good work**, and **increasing in the knowledge of God**; Vs 11 **Strengthened** with all might, according to his glorious power, unto all patience and longsuffering with **joyfulness**; 12 **Giving thanks** unto the Father, which hath made us meet to be partakers of the inheritance of the saints in light:"* [Emphasis added]

As a Princess to the Throne of Grace, you should walk in a way that is pleasing to the Lord; you should be serving the Lord and telling others about His wonderful love and grace; you should be developing a closer walk with God; you should let God strengthen you for what He calls you to do; you should be joyful in all situations; and you should give thanks to God.

Psalms 15:2 says, *"He that walketh uprightly, and worketh righteousness, and speaketh the truth in his heart."* And Romans 6:4, *"Therefore we are buried with him by baptism into death: that like as*

Christ was raised up from the dead by the glory of the Father, even so we also should walk in newness of life. "When you became a Princess to the Throne of Graces, God began working on your heart (the place where you make decisions) to begin changing you so that you would walk in *"newness of life."* This means that your life began to change as you read the Bible and started to realize what God expects. Your life began changing to please God. You began having conversations with God through prayer. Have you ever had that feeling that "I should not be here" or "I should not do this" or "I should not have acted this way?" This is the Holy Spirit gently guiding you to stand up straight or according to Psalms 15:2, *"walketh uprightly."* May you listen to the still small voice that shares with you how to stand up straight in the eyes of the King of Kings.

Tuesday:

No Slouching

As a Princess to the Throne of Grace, you want to please the King. You should have a desire to follow the commandments set forth in God's word and not slouch back into the things you did as an outsider to the throne. God's word is powerful and is full of examples of how those that follow God should live.

Read Galatians 5:16-26.

Slouching can be following what we want to do instead of doing what God commands us to do. When we do this we sin against God. This can be a sin such as adultery (a married person being unfaithful to their spouse), fornication (sexual impurity), uncleanness (impurity), lasciviousness (conduct shocking to public decency, a wanton violence), idolatry (service or worship of an idol), witchcraft (magic, sorcery, enchantment), hatred (enmity, hostility, alienation), variance (a readiness to quarrel), emulations (eagerness, zeal, jealousy, red-hot), wrath (outburst of anger), strife (ambition, rivalry, self-seeking), seditions (causing division, dissension), heresies (a self-chosen opinion), envyings (envy, a grudge, spite), murders (killing someone), drunkenness (deep drinking of alcohol), and revellings (riotous parties or parties with heavy drinking).

As a Princess to the Throne, our actions are being watched. Paul warns in Philippians 3:16-21, *"Nevertheless, whereto we have already attained, let us walk by the same rule, let us mind the same thing. 17 Brethren, be followers together of me, and mark them which walk so as ye have us for an ensample. 18 (For many walk, of whom I have told you often, and now tell you even weeping, that they are the enemies of the cross of Christ: 19 Whose end is destruction, whose God is their belly, and whose glory is in their shame, who mind earthly things.) 20 For our conversation is in heaven; from whence also we look for the Saviour, the Lord Jesus Christ: 21 Who shall change our vile body, that it may be fashioned like unto his glorious body, according to the working whereby he is able even to subdue all things unto himself."*

We have to be careful not to slouch. God wants to give us the fruits of the spirit as mentioned in Galations 5:22-23 following verse 25 to *"walk in the Spirit."* Proverbs 13:20 also warns against hanging out with the wrong friends, *"He that walketh with wise men shall be wise: but a companion of fools shall be destroyed."* Hanging with the wrong crowd will pull you down, instead of lifting you up.

James 1:22-25 says, *"But be ye doers of the word, and not hearers only, deceiving your own selves. 23 For if any be a hearer of the word, and not a doer, he is like unto a man beholding his natural face in a glass: 24 For he beholdeth himself, and goeth his way, and straightway forgetteth what manner of man he was. 25 But whoso looketh into the perfect law of liberty, and continueth therein, he being not a forgetful hearer, but a doer of the work, this man shall be blessed in his deed."*

In an effort not to slouch, the King demands that you apply the truths to your life. You cannot just hear what the Bible says; you deceive yourself if you choose not to be a doer of the word.

How does God want you to apply this message to your life?

_____

_____

_____

_____

_____

Wednesday:

Wave and Smile

As a princess, you are in the eye of the public. You are expected to smile and wave at others.

Read Ephesians 5:1-21.

Striking how similar the message is to the church at Ephesus. Verse 2, *"And walk in love, as Christ also hath loved us, and hath given **himself for us an offering and a sacrifice to God for a sweetsmelling savour.**"* [Emphasis added] How often do we offer ourselves as a sacrifice that is pleasing unto God as a *"sweetsmelling savour?"* As a Princess to the Throne of Grace, we are not to get caught up in the things of this world. Verse 3 states, *"let it not be **once** named among you."* [Emphasis added] This can be a challenge as we daily sacrifice our wants, desires, and sinful ways to be more Christ like. Hebrews 12:1-7 says, *"Wherefore seeing we also are compassed about with so great a cloud of witnesses, let us lay aside every weight, and the **sin which doth so easily beset us**, and **let us run with patience the race that is set before us**, 2 Looking unto Jesus the author and finisher of our faith; who for the joy that was set before him endured the cross, despising the shame, and is set down at the right hand of the throne of God. 3 For consider him that endured such contradiction of sinners against himself, lest ye be wearied and faint in your minds. 4 Ye have not yet resisted unto blood, striving against sin. 5 And ye have forgotten the exhortation which speaketh unto you as unto children, My son, **despise not thou the chastening of the Lord, nor faint when thou art rebuked of him**: 6 For whom the Lord loveth he chasteneth, and scourgeth every son whom he receiveth. 7 If ye endure chastening, **God dealeth with you as with sons** [daughters]; for what son [daughters] is he whom the father chasteneth not?"* [Emphasis added]

God loves you more than you can even imagine. He sent Jesus to die on the cross, so He would see His son's righteousness instead of our sin. Jesus said in John 8:12, *"Then spake Jesus again unto them, saying, I am the light of the world: he that followeth me shall not walk in darkness, but shall have the light of life."* In John 11:9-10, *"Jesus answered, Are there not twelve hours in the day? If any man walk in the day, he stumbleth not, because he seeth the light of this world. 10 But if a man walk in the night, he stumbleth, because there is no light in him."* Keeping your focus on Christ will keep you from stumbling as you smile and wave.

How can you keep your focus on Christ?

_____

_____

_____

_____

_____

Thursday:

Watch Where You Are Going

Read 2 Thessalonians 3:6-15.

Verse 6, *"Now we command you, ... from every brother that walketh disorderly,"* verse 7, *"For yourselves know how ye ought to follow us: for we behaved not ourselves disorderly among you;"* verse 9, *"to make ourselves an ensample"* verse 10, *"that if any would not work, neither should he eat."* Verse 11, *"busybodies"* according to the HELPS Word Studies is "to *fixate* on what *others* are doing, instead of doing what *the person himself* is supposed to do" Verse 13, *"be not weary in well doing."*

Psalm 1:1-3, *"Blessed is the man that walketh not in the counsel of the ungodly, nor standeth in the way of sinners, nor sitteth in the seat of the scornful. 2 But his delight is in the law of the LORD; and in his law doth he meditate day and night. 3 And he shall be like a tree planted by the rivers of water, that bringeth forth his fruit in his season; his leaf also shall not wither; and whatsoever he doeth shall prosper."*

Who are the ungodly?

_____

_____

This means "wicked" according to the *Strong's Concordance.*

How do we know we are in places that we should not be?

_____

_____

_____

_____

Psalms 1:1 states this is done by studying God's law and meditating on it.

The Bible also warns in 1 Thessalonians 5:22 to, *"Abstain from all appearance of evil."* This would include places where others might think "why is she going there" or "she acts like a Christian, so what is she doing here" or "if she can do this, so can I." As a Princess to the Throne of Grace, you have a great responsibility in advancing the kingdom of Christ. The Bible also warns in 1 Corinthians 10:12-13, *"Wherefore let him that thinketh he standeth **take heed lest he fall**. 13 There hath no temptation taken you but such as is common to man: but God is faithful, who will not suffer you to be **tempted above that ye are able**; but will with the temptation also make a way to escape, that ye may be able to bear it."* [Emphasis added] There will be times in your life you are tempted to go places or end up somewhere that is not pleasing to the King. Remember, God is with you to guide you and provide a way out. Titus 2:11-12 says, *"For the grace of God that bringeth salvation hath appeared to all men, 12 Teaching us that, **denying ungodliness and worldly lusts**, we should live soberly* [of a sound mind], *righteously* [justly], *and godly* [piously, religiously-having or showing a dutiful spirit of reverence for God or an earnest wish to fulfill religious obligations], *in this present world;"* [Definitions and emphasis added]

What does the media tell you about places that are ungodly?

———————————————————————

———————————————————————

———————————————————————

———————————————————————

———————————————————————

The messages include drinking is fun, dressing a certain way makes you desirable and you fit in by what you do or do not do. How can you live *"soberly, righteously and godly"* in today's world?

_____

_____

_____

_____

_____

Friday:

Keep Your Eyes on the King

Genesis 17:1, *"And when Abram was ninety years old and nine, the LORD appeared to Abram, and said unto him, I am the Almighty God; walk before me, and be thou perfect."*

Read Colossians 3:1-10.

How do you *"seek those things which are above?"*

_____

_____

_____

_____

How do you *"set your affection on things above?"*

_____

_____

_____

_____

What does verse 5-9 tell us to avoid?

_____

_____

_____

_____

Are they similar to the list from Tuesday? What other words do you need to review so you get the full meaning out of the verse?

Then, verse 10 tells us, *"And has put on the new man, which is renewed in knowledge after the image of him that created him."* We can put on the new man through Christ. 1 John 1:9 tells us, *"if we confess our sins he is faithful and just to forgive us."*

Romans 8:8-13 speaks to the importance of pleasing the King. *"So then they that are in the flesh cannot please God. 9 But ye are not in the flesh, but in the Spirit, if so be that the Spirit of God dwell in you. Now if any man have not the Spirit of Christ, he is none of his. 10 And if Christ be in you, the body is dead because of sin; but the Spirit is life because of righteousness. 11 But if the Spirit of him that raised up Jesus from the dead dwell in you, he that raised up Christ from the dead shall also quicken your mortal bodies by his Spirit that dwelleth in you. 12 Therefore, brethren, we are debtors, not to the flesh, to live after the flesh. 13 For if ye live after the flesh, ye shall die: but if ye through the Spirit do mortify the deeds of the body, ye shall live."* Another verse that speaks to this is Philippians 4:13 in that, *"Christ strengthens us."* We cannot live in the Spirit without daily prayer, Bible study, and building a relationship with the King of Kings.

Do you have your eyes on the King, Princess?

_____

_____

How can you apply these verses to your life?

_____

_____

_____

_____

_____

Saturday:
Walk with Poise and Grace

Princess, you are called to walk with poise and grace. Psalms 84:11, *"For the LORD God is a sun and shield: the LORD will give grace and glory: no good thing will he withhold from them that walk uprightly."* Through Christ, you can be strengthened to walk in elegance and grace before a righteous God. Only through the blood of Christ can you have this relationship. Christ's sacrifice on the cross gives us the access to the throne to be a Princess to the King. Galatians 4:1-7, *"Now I say, That the heir, as long as he is a child, differeth nothing from a servant, though he be lord of all; 2 But is under tutors and governors until the time appointed of the father. 3 Even so we, when we were children, were in bondage under the elements of the world: 4 But when the fulness of the time was come, God sent forth his Son, made of a woman, made under the law, 5 To redeem them that were under the law, that we might receive the adoption of sons. 6 And because ye are sons, God hath sent forth the Spirit of his Son into your hearts, crying, Abba, Father. 7 Wherefore thou art no more a servant, but a son; and if a son, then an heir of God through Christ."* Christ is calling us to walk in a new fashion. Read Ephesians 2:1-10.

What does it tell you?

_____

_____

_____

_____

We once walked in our own will doing our own things, *"but GOD"* [This is great stuff] in His mercy with *"great love"* has saved us by grace through Christ. We will be with Christ Jesus in heavenly places, making us a Princess to the Throne of Grace. In verse 7, *"That in the ages to come he might shew the exceeding riches of his grace in his kindness toward us through Christ Jesus."* God gave us this perfect gift, so no one could brag on what they had done to merit the Kingdom. Lastly in verse 10, *"For we are his workmanship, created in Christ Jesus unto good works, which God hath before ordained that we should walk in them."* Christ is our example of how we are to live on this Earth with poise and grace. Ephesians 4:1 says, *"I therefore, the prisoner of the Lord, beseech you that ye walk worthy of the vocation wherewith ye are called,…."* What is your vocation?

As a child of the King, you are called to the vocation [occupation] of Princess. Ephesians 4:2-7 states that this is done *"with all lowliness* [humility, lowliness of mind, modesty] *and meekness* [mildness, gentleness, kindness], *with longsuffering* [patience, waiting a long time without showing anger], *forbearing* [I endure, bear with, have patience with, suffer, admit, persist] *one another in love; 3 Endeavouring to keep the unity of the Spirit in the bond of peace. 4 There is one body, and one Spirit, even as ye are called in one hope of your calling; 5 One Lord, one faith, one baptism, 6 One God and Father of all, who is above all, and through all, and in you all. 7 But unto every one of us is given grace according to the measure of the gift of Christ."* [Definitions added]

You should be humble, kind, loving, gentle, and patient. These are only achieved through walking daily with Jesus Christ by reading the Bible, prayer, and meditation on God's word As a princess you will make choices minute by minute. Am I going to do what God wants or am I going to do what makes me feel good? Colossians 4:5-6 says to, *"Walk in wisdom toward them that are without, redeeming the time. 6 Let your speech be alway with grace, seasoned with salt, that ye may know how ye ought to answer every man."* As you go about your day, how is your conversation? Do others know by your walk that you are a believer? Do you look so much like your peers that no one would know?

_____

_____

_____

_____

_____

How can you apply the truths of God's word today?

_____

_____

_____

_____

Sunday:

Walk in the Light

In preparation for a day of worship, ask God to show you areas of your life that need to be changed, submitted to God, and how to encourage others within the fellowship of believers.

Psalms 13:1-4, "(A Psalm of David.) *LORD, who shall abide in thy tabernacle? who shall dwell in thy holy hill? 2 He that walketh uprightly, and worketh righteousness, and speaketh the truth in his heart. 3 He that backbiteth not with his tongue, nor doeth evil to his neighbour, nor taketh up a reproach against his neighbour. 4 In whose eyes a vile person is contemned; but he honoureth them that fear the LORD. He that sweareth to his own hurt, and changeth not.*"

Father, help me to abide in you that I might walk upright, follow your commands, and shine for you. Help my heart be filled with your truth and grace that my actions would show Jesus Christ in my heart. Today, may I reverence you and listen to the truth presented throughout the day that I may be willing to change whatever you show me. Amen

What did God show me today?

_____

_____

_____

_____

What areas of my life do I need to submit to God?

_____

_____

_____

How can I be a blessing to others or encourage other believers today?

_____

_____

_____

_____

_____

How can I be a blessing to others or encourage others this week?

_____

_____

_____

_____

_____

Talking Like a Princess

Monday:

Speak Clearly

Have you ever had trouble speaking in a crowd? Prior to becoming a princess, you may have been quite invisible to many. As a Princess, you have entered into the spotlight of the public eye. A Princess to the Throne of Grace will need to speak clearly, holding her head high in the confidence of the ability given by the King.

Read 1 Peter 3:10-22.

What is the King telling us in this passage?

_____

_____

_____

_____

_____

As you started reading the passage, did you notice what the passage said about not using our tongue for *"evil"* and with our mouth we should speak no *"guile."* Did this word cause you to pause? What is "guile?" According to Meriam Webster, it is "the act of causing someone to accept as true or valid what is false or invalid" or "the quality of being dishonest or misleading." What about *"eschew?"* This means to "fall away from" or "turn away" evil. What is evil? Evil is defined as "morally reprehensible" or morally disapproving. God sets the standard. Verse 15-17 states, *"But **sanctify** the Lord God in your hearts: and **be ready always to give an answer to every man that asketh you a reason of the hope that is in you** with meekness* [gentleness] *and fear* [reverence]: *16 Having a good conscience; that, whereas they speak evil of you, as of evildoers, they may be ashamed that falsely accuse your good conversation in Christ."* [Emphasis added and definitions from the *Strong's Concordance*] Because you are a Princess to the Throne of Grace, you should be able to speak clearly to anyone that asks you about how you became a princess or why you are different than before you became a princess. The Bible also tells us it is not just what we say, but how we say it. As you share your story with others, some will reject the King of Kings. This may cause them to make fun of you or get mad or not want to be friends because of your new status. God said in Verse 17, *"For it is better, if the will of God be so, that ye suffer for well doing, than for evil doing."* For just as Christ suffered for you and God has been longsuffering [patient or forbearance, which is "a refraining from the enforcement of something (as a debt, right, or obligation) that is due" according to Meriam Webster], as a Princess to the Throne of Grace you should give an answer and be patient and forgiving with those that do not want to be part of the royal family.

James 1:23-27 says, *"For if any be a hearer of the word, and not a doer, he is like unto a man beholding his natural face in a glass: 24 For he beholdeth himself, and goeth his way, and straightway forgetteth what manner of man he was. 25 But whoso looketh into the perfect law of liberty, and continueth therein, he being **not a forgetful hearer, but a doer of the work**, this man shall be blessed in his deed. 26 If any man among you **seem to be religious**, and **bridleth not his tongue**, but* *deceiveth his own heart, this man's **religion is vain**. 27 Pure religion and undefiled before God and the Father is this, To visit the fatherless and widows in their affliction, and to keep himself unspotted from the world."* [Emphasis added] The Bible tells us not to be just a hearer of the word, but there should be a change in our speech. We can seem to be religious in church on Sunday or Wednesday or during church activities. God knows your heart, your thoughts, and hears every word that you think or say. God is interested in your character or what you do when no one is watching. May your speech be clear of ungodly things. May you learn to bridle your tongue. Have you ever been on a horse or seen a horse with a bridle? Attached to the bridle is a bit that goes into the horse's mouth, which allows the rider to guide the horse in the direction you want to go. Sometimes, one has to change to different bits to get the horse to respond. God wants you to bridle your tongue. God also wants you to be able to share God's love and what Christ did with others. As a Princess to the Throne of Grace you need to be able to speak clearly and without fear, as well as with patience and reverence.

How are you doing, Princess? Do you speak clearly for the Kingdom?

_____

_____

What can you improve upon?

_____

_____

_____

_____

_____

Choose Your Words Carefully

1 Cor. 2:3-10 states, *"And I was with you in weakness, and in fear, and in much trembling. 4 And my* **speech and my preaching was not with enticing words of man's wisdom**, *but in demonstration of the Spirit and of power: 5 That your faith should not stand in the wisdom of men, but in the power of God. 6 Howbeit we speak wisdom among them that are perfect: yet not the wisdom of this world, nor of the princes of this world, that come to nought: 7* **But we speak the wisdom of God in a mystery, even the hidden wisdom, which God ordained before the world unto our glory:** *8 Which none of the princes of this world knew: for had they known it, they would not have crucified the Lord of glory. 9 But as it is written, Eye hath not seen, nor ear heard, neither have entered into the heart of man, the things which God hath prepared for them that love him. 10 But God hath revealed them unto us by his Spirit: for the Spirit searcheth all things, yea, the deep things of God."* [Emphasis added] Paul was letting the church at Corinth know that his speech was not with man's wisdom, encouraging us to stand in the power of God. Romans 14:19 tells us to edify [to instruct and improve especially in moral and religious knowledge] one another. Philippians 2:11-15 says, *"And that every tongue should confess that Jesus Christ is Lord, to the glory of God the Father. 12 Wherefore, my beloved, as ye have always obeyed,* **not as in my presence only**, *but now much more* **in my absence**, *work out your own salvation with fear and trembling. 13 For it is God which worketh in you both to will and to do of his good pleasure. 14 Do all things without murmurings* [grumbling] *and disputings* [a calculation, reasoning, thought, plotting]: *15 That ye may be blameless and harmless, the sons of God, without rebuke, in the midst of a crooked and perverse nation, among whom ye shine as lights in*

the world;" [Definition and emphasis added] Paul recognized that the Philippians were professing Christ not just in his presence, but in his absence. How is your profession of Christ? Are you full of grumbling and disputing? Maybe you are not professing Christ when you are not at church or with your friends from church?

Read Psalms 12.

What does it say about your speech?

_____

_____

_____

_____

_____

Flattery to get what you want, thinking that you are above others, or speaking of yourself is of concern, Princess. Be careful not to talk of yourself throughout your conversation or be full of flatter for another purpose. What is flattery? It is along the lines of saying nice things to someone else for a complement in return or to get something that you want. "Mom, I love you. You look beautiful today. Can I go do _____?" Fill in the blank.

Psalms 10:4-7 says, *"The wicked, through the pride of his countenance, will not seek after God: God is not in all his thoughts. 5 His ways are always grievous; thy judgments are far above out of his sight: as for all his enemies, he puffeth at them. 6 He hath said in his heart, I shall not be moved: for I shall never be in adversity. 7 His mouth is **full of cursing and deceit and fraud: under his tongue is mischief and vanity.**"* [Emphasis added]

God also commands us in Exodus 20:6-7, *"And shewing mercy unto thousands of them that love me, and keep my commandments. 7 Thou shalt not take the **name of the LORD thy God in vain**; for* *the LORD will not hold him guiltless that taketh his name in vain."* [Emphasis added] What does this mean? In our culture today, using God's name without respect is continual. You hear people say Jesus Christ without calling on him out of love and respect. You see OMG in texts, on t-shirts, to show excitement, and on various products. Some of you may say, well I meant it as OM Gosh. I have even seen some use OM Gosh. Have you ever wondered why we don't say OM Budda or OM Ala? Be careful Princess, as this is a slippery slope with disrespect for your King. Choose your words carefully.

1 Corinthians 4:18-21 provides an example of speech that was arrogant. *"Now some are puffed up* [arrogant, proud], *as though I would not come to you. 19 But I will come to you shortly, if the Lord will, and will know, not the speech of them which are puffed up, but the power. 20 For the kingdom of God is not in word, but in power. 21 What will ye? shall I come unto you with a rod, or in love, and in the spirit of meekness* [mildness or kindness]?" [Definition added from *Strong's Concordance*] What is arrogance? *Meriam Webster* defines it as "exaggerating or disposed to exaggerate one's own worth or importance often by an overbearing manner." We should not think more highly of ourselves than others. We are saved by God's grace. We are a princess only through Christ. We need to remember our place. Romans 16:17-19 says, *"Now I beseech you, brethren, mark them which cause divisions* [dissention] *and offences* [a snare, stumbling-block] *contrary to the doctrine which ye have learned; and **avoid them**. 18 For they that are such serve not our Lord Jesus Christ, but their own belly; and by good words and fair speeches deceive the hearts of the simple. 19 For your obedience is come abroad unto all men. I am glad therefore on your behalf: but yet I would have you wise unto that which is good, and simple concerning evil."* Our speech should not be filled with dissention [contentious quarreling] or "likely to

cause disagreement or argument." [Meriam Webster definition of dissention and contentious]

1 Corinthians 13:1 tells us that, *"Though I speak with the tongues of men and of angels, and have not charity* [love]*, I am become as sounding brass, or a tinkling cymbal."* [Definition added] 1 Peter 3:8-9 says, *"Finally, be ye all of one mind, having compassion one of another, love as brethren, be pitiful, be courteous: 9 Not rendering evil for evil, or railing for railing: but contrariwise blessing; knowing that ye are thereunto called, that ye should inherit a blessing."* Our words should be edifying, loving, and full of compassion. Our words should not be arrogant, proud, contentious, quarreling, or taking the Lord's name in vain. If it feels good to say it, it is probably not what God wants you to say.

How are you choosing your word? Are you saying what feels good? Are you tearing others down with your words?

_____

_____

How do they sound?

_____

_____

_____

_____

Think Before You Speak

As a Princess to the Throne of Grace, you need to think before you speak. Ecclesiastes 5:3 says, *"For a dream cometh through the multitude of business; and a fool's voice [is known] by multitude of words."* My husband has often said "more words equal more problems." Proverbs 13:3 says, *"He that keepeth his mouth keepeth his life: but he that openeth wide his lips shall have destruction."* As a princess you will need to have control of your mouth, speak less, and listen more.

Ecclesiastes 10:12-15 says, *"The words of a wise man's mouth [are] gracious; but the lips of a fool will swallow up himself. 13 The beginning of the words of his mouth [is] foolishness: and the end of his talk [is] mischievous madness. 14 A fool also is **full of words**: a man cannot tell what shall be; and what shall be after him, who can tell him? 15 The labour of the foolish wearieth every one of them, because he knoweth not how to go to the city."* [Emphasis added] Have you ever been around someone that talked way too much? James has much to say about the tongue and our words.

Read James 3:1-10.

What is it saying?

_____

_____

_____

_____

_____

We offend with our words, our tongue is evil if not bridled, and our mouth should not be full of cursing and blessings. How are your words?

How do you carefully choose your words?

_____

_____

_____

_____

_____

2 Timothy 2:15-19 tells us to, *"Study to shew thyself approved unto God, a workman that needeth not to be ashamed, rightly dividing the word of truth. 16 But shun profane* [relating or devoted to that which is not sacred or biblical; secular rather than religious, unspiritual, godless, worldly] *and vain babblings* [empty disputing, worthless babble chatter, empty talk]: *for they will increase unto more ungodliness. 17And their word will eat as doth a canker: of whom is Hymenaeus and Philetus; 18 Who concerning the truth have erred, saying that the resurrection is past already; and overthrow the faith of some. 19 Nevertheless the foundation of God standeth sure, having this seal, The Lord knoweth them that are his. And, Let every one that nameth the name of Christ depart from iniquity* [sin]." [*Dictionary and Strong's Concordance*]

Are you thinking before you speak?

What do you struggle with in this area?

_____

_____

_____

_____

_____

Thursday:

Your Words are Recorded

Romans 14:10-17, *"But why dost thou judge thy brother? or why dost thou set at nought thy brother? for we shall all stand before the judgment seat of Christ. 11 For it is written, As I live, saith the Lord, every knee shall bow to me, and every tongue shall confess to God. 12* **So then every one of us shall give account of himself to God.** *13 Let us not therefore judge one another any more: but judge this rather, that* **no man put a stumblingblock or an occasion to fall in his brother's way.** *14 I know, and am persuaded by the Lord Jesus, that there is nothing unclean of itself: but to him that esteemeth any thing to be unclean, to him it is unclean. 15 But if thy brother be grieved with thy meat, now walkest thou not charitably. Destroy not him with thy meat, for whom Christ died. 16 Let not then your good be evil spoken of: 17 For the kingdom of God is not meat and drink; but righteousness, and peace, and joy in the Holy Ghost."* [Emphasis added] Everyone of us will give an account for our words. As a princess, you should make sure that your words or actions are not a stumbling block for others.

Read Matthew 12:31-37.

Jesus said, *"But I say unto you, That every idle word that men shall speak, they shall give account thereof in the day of judgment."* If someone was following you every day with a microphone, would you choose your words more carefully? Princess, your words are being recorded. What do you need to change?

_____
_____
_____
_____
_____

How would they sound?

_____

_____

_____

_____

_____

What emotions do they show? Are you choosing words that God will be pleased with during your day?

_____

_____

_____

_____

_____

Are you confessing your poor choices when you choose unwisely? Are you asking forgiveness of the other person?

_____

_____

_____

_____

_____

Friday:

Show Respect to the King

In 2 Corinthians 7:1, *"Having therefore these promises* [God's promises of the New Testament], *dearly beloved, let us cleanse ourselves from all filthiness* [staining, defilement, pollution] *of the flesh* [human nature] *and spirit* [breathe], *perfecting* [I complete, accomplish, perfect] *holiness* [sanctification] *in the fear* [reverence] *of God."* [Definitions from *Strong's Concordance*] In this chapter, the Apostle Paul begins with an address or communication urging the believers at Corinth to live sanctified or set apart out of reverence or respect to the King. Why, you may ask? Paul answers this in the first part of the verse, *"having therefore these promises."* Paul urged fellow believers to live in a way that showed respect to the one that died for their sins, because of the great promises that they have in Christ.

As we continue to talk like a princess, we should honor the King of Kings through our communication.

Read Psalm 89:1-18.

What words does the Psalmist use to characterize God?

_____

_____

_____

Some of the characteristics of God mentioned in this passage are faithful, merciful, to be feared, to be reverenced, strong, deserving praise, ruler, just, judge, truth, king, and defender. As a Princess to the Throne of Grace, our communication in God should show confidence in the almighty power that He has in the world around us. We should not be communicating like there is no hope. The King of Kings, who *"rulest the raging of the sea,"* is in control.

Verse 15-18 is for us as daughters of the King. *"Blessed is the people that know the joyful sound: they shall walk, O LORD,* **in the light of thy countenance.** *16 In thy name shall* **they rejoice all the day:** *and* **in thy righteousness** *shall they be exalted. 17 For thou art* **the glory of their strength:** *and in thy favour our horn shall be exalted. 18 For* **the LORD is our defence**; *and the Holy One of Israel is our king."* [Emphasis added]

How is your communication throughout the day? Are you walking with the light of the Lord's countenance? Are you rejoicing all the day? Are you depending on your own righteousness? I am a good girl by following the rules, obeying my parents, and doing and saying the right things in public. The King of Kings is your source of righteousness. We are all sinners saved by grace (I trust you have asked the Lord to save you). Sometimes as Christians, we become self-righteous comparing ourselves with other believers instead of focusing on who God wants us to be through Him. Do you let Christ strengthen you daily? Is He your defense? Is God your first resort or your last when everything else you have tried has failed? Are you worried, fearful, angry, and anxious? As a Princess to the Throne of Grace, first God loves you unconditionally. We all sin and fall back into old habits. Call sin, sin. Confess and turn from it. Second, He wants you to depend on Him as your source of strength. Third, our flesh is hard to fight without relying on strength from Christ.

What area of your life does the King want you to give to him?

_____

_____

_____

_____

_____

Saturday:

Be Seasoned with Grace

Proverbs 7:1 says, *"My son [daughter in this case], keep my words…"*

Read Psalm 78:31-39.

What is the Psalmist saying?

_____

_____

_____

_____

_____

God was angry with Israel. They had sinned against God. They were flattering with their words and lying with their tongue, because their hearts were not right. Then, Verse 38 says, *"But he [God], being full of compassion, forgave their iniquity, and destroyed them not: yea, many a time turned he his anger away, and did not stir up all his wrath."* [Added for clarity] God is full of compassion and is faithful to forgive us when we mess up.

Colossians 4:1-6 says, *"Masters, give unto your servants that which is just and equal; knowing that ye also have a Master in heaven. 2 Continue in prayer, and watch in the same with thanksgiving; 3 Withal praying also for us, that God would open unto us a door of utterance, to speak the mystery of Christ, for which I am also in bonds: 4 That I may make it manifest, as I ought to speak. 5 Walk in wisdom toward them that are without, redeeming the time. 6 Let your speech be alway with grace, seasoned with salt, that ye may know how ye ought to answer every man."*

As a Princess to the Throne of Grace, our words are seasoned with grace as we spend time building a relationship with Christ and behaving in a way pleasing to the King. The King wants you to walk in wisdom through studying His word, continuing in pray, and with a thankful heart, so you will be ready to share Christ with others.

How is your speech? Is it seasoned with salt? Are you ready to answer?

_____

_____

_____

_____

_____

Sunday:

Be a Sweet Savor

In preparation for a day of worship, ask God to show you areas of your life that need to be changed, submitted to God, and how to encourage others within the fellowship of believers.

2 Corinthians 2:15, *"For we are unto God a sweet savour of Christ, in them that are saved, and in them that perish:"*

Father, help me to worship you today. May my offerings be a sweet savor to You. Show me the things in my life that I need to change. Give me scripture to cling to in order to make these changes. Encourage me today through your word during the services. Thank you for loving me, Father, and wanting the best for me.

What did God show me today?

_____

_____

_____

_____

What areas of my life do I need to submit to God?

_____

_____

_____

_____

119

How can I be a blessing to others or encourage other believers today?

_____

_____

_____

_____

_____

How can I be a blessing to others or encourage others this week?

_____

_____

_____

_____

_____

Heir to the Throne

Blessings of Inheritance

The word bless is listed 463 times in the Bible. As we begin looking at the blessings of your inheritance, write down some of the ways the King has blessed you.

_____

_____

_____

As a Princess to the Throne of Grace, we are blessed through salvation and the promise that we will not spend eternity separated from the King of Kings. Hebrews 1:1-4, *"God, who at sundry times and in divers manners spake in time past unto the fathers by the prophets, 2 Hath in these last days spoken unto us by his Son, whom **he hath appointed heir of all things**, by whom also he made the worlds; 3 Who being the brightness of his glory, and the express image of his person, and **upholding all things by the word of his power**, when he had by himself purged our sins, sat down **on the right hand of the Majesty on high**; 4 Being made so much better than the angels, as he hath by inheritance obtained a more excellent name than they."* [Emphasis added]

121

Christ is the blessing of our inheritance. Romans 8:17-18, *"And if children, then heirs; heirs of God, and joint-heirs with Christ; if so be that we suffer with him, that we may be also glorified together. 18 For I reckon that the sufferings of this present time are not worthy to be compared with the glory which shall be revealed in us."* Revelation 22:12-14, *"And, behold, I come quickly; and my reward is with me, to give every man according as his work shall be. 13 I am Alpha and Omega, the beginning and the end, the first and the last. 14 Blessed are they that do his commandments, that they may have right to the tree of life, and may enter in through the gates into the city."* The blessings of our inheritance will come with Christ's return; however, God the Father continues to bless us as we live for Him. John 15:16, *"Ye have not chosen me, but I have chosen you, and ordained you, that ye should go and **bring forth fruit, and that your fruit should remain**: that **whatsoever ye shall ask of the Father in my name, he may give it you.**"* [Emphasis added] The King wants to bless you. He has given you the Holy Spirit as a gift. Romans 8:24-28, *"For we are saved by hope: but hope that is seen is not hope: for what a man seeth, why doth he yet hope for? 25 But if we hope for that we see not, **then do we with patience wait for it**. 26 Likewise the Spirit also **helpeth our infirmities**: for we know not what we should pray for as we ought: but **the Spirit itself maketh intercession for us** with groanings which cannot be uttered. 27 And he that searcheth the hearts knoweth what is the mind of the Spirit, because he maketh **intercession for the saints according to the will of God**. 28 And we know that all things work together for good to them that love God, to them who are the called according to his purpose."* [Emphasis added] The Spirit makes intercession for you according to the will of God. Know princess that the King loves you beyond measure.

Read Psalm 115.

What is the Psalmist saying in this passage?

_____

_____

_____

We should give glory to God for mercy and truth. God is not like the idols of man. He speaks, sees, and hears. As a princess, we are called to trust in the Lord as He is our help and shield. The King is mindful of us and blesses us as we fear him and reverence him. *Matthew Henry's Full Commentary* on verse 14 states, *"The Lord shall increase you. Whom God blesses he increases; that was one of the earliest and most ancient blessings, Be fruitful and multiply. God's blessing gives an increase—increase in number, building up the family—increase in wealth, adding to the estate and honour—especially an increase in spiritual blessings, with the increasings of God. He will bless you with the increase of knowledge and wisdom, of grace, holiness, and joy; those are blessed indeed whom God thus increases, who are made wiser and better, and fitter for God and heaven. It is promised that this shall be,..."* Our King made the heavens and earth, so he has full authority to bless us for His glory.

Do you trust the blessings of the King?

_____

_____

_____

Have you ever heard it said that God answers our request either "Yes," "No," or "I have something better for you?" Our culture is to get what you want now with instant reward. The King of Kings is saying, "Do you trust me to do what is best for you?" This is part of the blessings of being a princess. You have a King that is mindful of you.

He has a purpose for you and will fill you with wisdom, grace, holiness, joy, spiritual blessings, and equip you to do what he asks of you.

Now, make a list of the blessings God has given you? How does this compare with your list at the beginning? Do you recognize more blessings that you have as a Princess to the Throne of Grace?

_____

_____

_____

Be Wise in Your Inheritance

Proverbs 15:13-16, *"A merry heart maketh a cheerful countenance: but by sorrow of the heart the spirit is broken. 14 The heart of him that hath understanding seeketh knowledge: but the mouth of fools feedeth on foolishness. 15 All the days of the afflicted are evil: but he that is of a merry heart hath a continual feast. 16 Better is little with the fear of the LORD than great treasure and trouble therewith."*

Read Luke 15:11-32.

What did the younger son want?

_____

_____

What did he do?

_____

_____

What happened when the money ran out?

_____

_____

What happened when he came to his senses?

_____

_____

Jesus shared this parable about two sons often referred to as the story of the Prodigal Son. The younger of the two wanted his inheritance early, so the father divided his wealth. The younger son went into a far country and wasted his inheritance on *"riotous* (meaning wasteful, reckless, or uncontrolled) *living."* His money began to run out. As a Jewish boy, he ended up eating the feed intended for the pigs (an unclean animal). He had hit bottom. He came to his senses knowing that his father's servants ate better with food to spare. He would return as a hired servant. His father was watching for him and saw him off in the distance. His father ran to him, kissed him, and had compassion on him. His father dressed him, had a feast for him, and celebrated his return. This father received him unto his own, not as a servant. Well, as you can imagine, this did not make the older son happy. In fact, he was extremely angry at his father for his grand welcoming of his younger brother. The father was rejoicing that the son was not dead or living a life of sin, but was alive and had returned.

This parable reminds us of lies from the Prince of this World. He will tempt you to go be wild and crazy in your youth, so you "can find yourself." Jesus spoke of this son to show us that there is redemption for us. Our King is always ready to receive us back unto himself, watching in anticipation for us to return home. He wants us to live and rejoices when we do not fall for the lies of this world. As a Princess to the Throne of Grace, there will be Princes, friends, and relatives that will attempt to persuade you to live a life that is not pleasing to the King. The younger son lost his inheritance and returned in humility to be a mere servant of his father. His father showed mercy in restoring him to the family. The son returned but not without scars from his past and consequences to his wasteful living. Be wise in your inheritance, Princess. Matthew 6:20-21, *"But lay up for yourselves treasures in heaven, where neither moth nor rust doth corrupt, and where thieves do not break through nor steal: 21 For where your treasure is, there will your heart be also."* The prodigal son found friends willing to spend his money, but none when the money ran out. Hebrews 11:25 discusses Moses and the choice that he made by *"Choosing rather to suffer affliction with the people of God, than to enjoy the pleasures of sin for a season."* Moses could have lived a life of great luxury as a son to Pharaoh, but he chose to live a life pleasing to God.

How about you, Princess? Are you living recklessly, on the edge of what you know God wants you to do? Are you choosing to live a life pleasing to God?

_____

_____

Jesus said in Luke 6:43-46, *"For a good tree bringeth not forth corrupt fruit; neither doth a corrupt tree bring forth good fruit. 44 For every tree is known by his own fruit. For of thorns men do not gather figs, nor of a bramble bush gather they grapes. 45 A good man out of the good treasure of his heart bringeth forth that which is good; and an evil man out of the evil treasure of his heart bringeth forth that which is evil: for of the abundance of the heart his mouth speaketh. 46 And why call ye me, Lord, Lord, and do not the things which I say?"* As a Princess to the Throne of Grace, you make choices every day to serve the King and follow His commandments or choose your own direction and move closer to the far away land. Riches and luxuries are not forbidden as we have many examples in the Bible of families that prospered as they lived a life pleasing to King. On the other hand, we also see examples of destruction as individuals, families, and communities made choices to live for themselves. Proverbs 8:10-11, *"Receive my instruction, and not silver; and knowledge rather than choice gold. 11 For wisdom is better than rubies; and all the things that may be desired are not to be compared to it."* Choose to be wise with your inheritance.

What is the King telling you as you reflect on what Jesus was teaching?

_____

_____

_____

_____

_____

How can you apply it today?

_____

_____

_____

_____

_____

Share Your Inheritance

In Mark 5, Jesus removed the unclean spirits from a man. After changing his life, Jesus said to him in verse 19, *"... Go home to thy friends, and tell them how great things the Lord hath done for thee, and hath had compassion on thee."* As a Princess to the Throne of Grace, you should share your story.

Matthew 28:18-20, *"And Jesus came and spake unto them, saying, All power is given unto me in heaven and in earth. 19 **Go ye therefore**, and teach all nations, baptizing them in the name of the Father, and of the Son, and of the Holy Ghost: 20 Teaching them to observe all things whatsoever I have commanded you: and, lo, I am with you alway, even unto the end of the world. Amen."* [Emphasis added]

Mark 16:15-16, *"And he [Jesus] said unto them, Go ye into all the world, and preach the gospel to every creature. 16 He that believeth and is baptized shall be saved..."* [Clarification added]

Read Acts 5:16-42.

Why were the apostles put in prison?

_____

_____

What did the angel of the Lord do in this passage?

_____

_____

What commandment were the apostles given?

_____

_____

What happened next?

_____

_____

How did Peter and the apostles answer the questioning?

_____

_____

Why were the apostles rejoicing in persecution?

_____

_____

_____

The Sadducees were angry that the apostles were healing and preaching the gospel, so they had the apostles put in prison. This could not stop the work of the Lord, as the angel of the Lord opened the prison doors. This came with a command to, *"Go, stand and speak in the temple to the people all the words of this life."* The apostles obeyed the command of the angel of the Lord and entered into the temple *"early in the morning, and taught."* Notice that they did not wait or delay the command of the Lord. The apostles were brought back for questioning, but did not want to create a scene. They were fearful for their life and concerned about being stoned. The Sadducees brought them before the council, questioning them regarding their teachings of the gospel. Peter and the apostles responded with the gospel. The council was eager to kill the apostles, but one spoke up. They agreed to beat them and let them go. The apostles departed, *"...rejoicing that they were counted worthy to suffer shame for his name. And daily in the temple, and in every house, they ceased not to teach and preach Jesus Christ."* Did you notice that the one person changed the outcome for the apostles? Did you notice that no matter what the apostles continued to share the gospel with others?

Romans 1:16-17 says, *"For I am not ashamed of the gospel of Christ: for it is the power of God unto salvation to every one that believeth; to the Jew first, and also to the Greek. 17 For therein is the righteousness of God revealed from faith to faith: as it is written, The just shall live by faith."*

Maybe you think you will say the wrong thing when sharing the gospel. Paul said in 1 Corinthians 2:1-7, *"And I, brethren, when I came to you, came **not with excellency of speech or of wisdom**, declaring unto you the testimony of God. 2 For I determined not to know any thing among you, save Jesus Christ, and him crucified. 3 And I was with you in weakness, and in fear, and in much trembling. 4 **And my speech and my preaching was not with enticing words of man's wisdom**, but in **demonstration of the Spirit and of power**: 5 That your faith should not stand in the wisdom of men, but in the power of God. 6 Howbeit we speak wisdom among them that are perfect: yet not the wisdom of this world, nor of the princes of this world, that come to nought: 7 But we speak the wisdom of God in a mystery, even the hidden wisdom, which God ordained before the world unto our glory:"* [Emphasis added] Paul said it is not about the words that we use. It is the power of God unto salvation.

Romans 10:14-15 says, *"How then shall they call on him in whom they have not believed? and how shall they believe in him of whom they have not heard? and how shall they hear without a preacher? 15 And how shall they preach, **except they be sent**? as it is written, **How beautiful are the feet of them that preach the gospel of peace, and bring glad tidings of good things!**"* [Emphasis added] As a Princess to the Throne of Grace, you should be sharing the gospel of peace with others. Are you sharing your inheritance with others? Are you eager to tell others about the King of Kings?

2 Corinthians 4:5-7, *"For we preach not ourselves, but Christ Jesus the Lord; and ourselves your servants for Jesus' sake. 6 For God,*

*who commanded the light to shine out of darkness, **hath shined in our hearts, to give the light of the knowledge of the glory of God in the face of Jesus Christ**. 7 But we have this treasure in earthen vessels, that the excellency of the power may be of God, and not of us."* [Emphasis added] The King of Kings has given us a new life. We should be ready to share our inheritance. Ask God to give you someone to share the gospel with this week?

_____
_____
_____
_____
_____

Grow In Your Inheritance

Jesus was speaking in Matthew 13:30 after discussing sowing (or planting) and said, *"Let both grow together until the harvest* [a time of gathering of those who are part of the Kingdom]: *and in the time of harvest I will say to the reapers, Gather ye together first the tares* [those caught up in sin], *and bind them in bundles to burn them* [consumed by fire]: *but gather the wheat into my barn* [those who know Christ]." Oh, Princess! I encourage you to grow in the grace of our Lord and King.

Read 2 Peter 3:1-18.

What should you be mindful of?

_____

_____

What is coming in the last days?

_____

_____

What is being referenced in verse 5-6?

_____

_____

What should we not be ignorant of?

_____

_____

What does verse 9 say about God's character?

_____

_____

What does God want for all of us?

_____

_____

What promise is made in verse 10?

_____

_____

How should God find us?

_____

_____

What should we beware of?

_____

_____

Write out verse 18:

_____

_____

_____

_____

_____

As a princess you should be mindful of the words and commandments given to us in God's word. In the last days, there will be those who scoff [to show contempt by derisive acts or language]. *Matthew Henry's Commentary* on verses 1-4 states, *"The purified minds of Christians are to be stirred up, that they may be active and lively in the work of holiness. There will be scoffers in the last days, under the gospel, men who make light of sin, and mock at salvation by Jesus Christ. One very principal article of our faith refers to what only has a promise to rest upon, and scoffers will attack it till our Lord is come."* Verse 5 and 6 are referring both to God creating the world and the great flood in the days of Noah. God will keep His promise, just as in the days of Noah. Noah was ridiculed for building the ark, when it had not rained on the earth. Just as God kept His promise to Noah, God will keep His promises to us regarding His return. As a Princess to the Throne of Grace, we should not be ignorant that God is not bound by time. God's character is revealed in verse 9 as he is longsuffering. God is *"not willing that any should perish, but that all should come to repentance."* Christ will also come when unexpected to receive His own, as *"a thief in the night."* God promised that this earth shall be burned up. Peter encourages us to be found faithful in *"all holy conversation and godliness"* and diligently looking for His return that *"ye may be found of him in peace, without spot, and blameless."* We should be sharing salvation with others until the return of our Lord, because he is longsuffering. As a princess, you should beware of those that are in error of the King's ways. Verses 16 goes on to say, *"As also in all his epistles* **[Paul]**, *speaking in them of these things* **[teachings of the gospel and truths of God's word]**; *in which are some things hard to be understood, which they that are unlearned* **[ignorant]** *and unstable* **[unreliable]** *wrest* **[perverted or twisted]**, *as they do also the other scriptures, unto their own destruction* **[ruin]**. [Clarification and definitions added based on *Strong's Concordance* and *Matthew Henry's Full Commentary*]. Verse 17 warns you not to fall away from your stedfastness and be led away by error. This is why it is critical that you as a Princess know what you believe from God's word, so you can withstand against those who are in error to the King. Verse 18 offers encouragement to, *"...grow in grace, and in the knowledge of our Lord and Saviour Jesus Christ. To him be glory both now and for ever. Amen."*

How do we grow in grace?

_____

_____

1 Peter 2:2-5 says, *"As newborn babes, **desire** the sincere milk of the **word**, that ye **may grow** thereby: 3 If so be **ye have tasted that the Lord is gracious**. 4 To whom coming, as unto a living stone, disallowed indeed of men, but **chosen of God, and precious**, 5 Ye also, as lively stones, are **built up** a spiritual house, an **holy priesthood**, to offer up **spiritual sacrifices**, acceptable to God by Jesus Christ."* [Emphasis added]

You grow in grace by reading and studying God's word, by developing a relationship with the King through conversation, by following His commandments, and by offering ourselves as a living sacrifice.

Are you growing in grace?

_____

_____

Write down one thing that could strengthen your relationship with the King of Kings?

_____

_____

_____

_____

_____

Invest in Your Inheritance

Ecclesiastes 3:11-14, *"He hath made every thing beautiful in his time: also he hath set the world in their heart, so that no man can find out the work that God maketh from the beginning to the end. 12 I know that there is no good in them, but for a man to rejoice, and to do good in his life. 13 And also that every man should eat and drink, and enjoy the good of all his labour, it is the gift of God. 14 I know that, whatsoever God doeth, it shall be for ever: nothing can be put to it, nor any thing taken from it: and God doeth it, that men should fear before him"* In Matthew 7:7-11, Jesus said, *"Ask, and it shall be given you; seek, and ye shall find; knock, and it shall be opened unto you: 8 For every one that asketh receiveth; and he that seeketh findeth; and to him that knocketh it shall be opened. 9 Or what man is there of you, whom if his son ask bread, will he give him a stone? 10 Or if he ask a fish, will he give him a serpent? 11 If ye then, being evil, know how to give good gifts unto your children, how much more shall your Father which is in heaven give good things to them that ask him?"* The King is perfect in wisdom, truth, power, love, and giving. Jesus was saying just as your earthly parents can give good gifts to their children, the King in His perfect love and wisdom will give good gift to him that ask. This does not mean that he will give you earthly treasure or luxuries, but will give you what you need.

The King also knows you in a very personal way. He loves you and has designed you for a purpose to share His love to others. He equips each of us differently as a Princess to the Throne of Grace.

Read Matthew 25:13-30.

How did the master choose to give talents to his servants?

_____

_____

What did the master say to the servant with five talents?

_____

_____

What did the master say to the servant with two talents?

_____

_____

What did the master say to the servant with one talent? Why?

_____

_____

Watch therefore, for ye know neither the day nor the hour wherein the Son of man cometh.

The talents were given based on their ability. The servant with five talents turned them into ten talents. The servant with two talents turned them into four. The servant with one talent hid it in the ground, not doing anything with the money. When the master returned, the servant who was given five talents presented ten talents. Verse 21 says *"His lord said unto him, Well done, thou good and faithful servant: thou hast been faithful over a few things, I will make thee ruler over many things: enter thou into the joy of thy lord."* The servant, who was given two talents, presented four talents. Verse 23 says *"His lord said unto him, Well done, good and faithful servant; thou hast been faithful over a few things, I will make thee ruler over many things: enter thou into the joy of thy lord."* The servant who hid his one talent was called wicked and lazy by his master, so the lord gave it to someone else.

Just as we are all unique and have various talents (no money as referred to above), the King wants us to use them according to what we have been given. The servant with two talents, who invested them wisely, received, *"Well done, thou good and faithful servant."* Romans 12:4-8, *"For as we have many members in one body, and all members have not the same office* [our eyes cannot decide to be feet]*: 5 So we, being many, are one body in Christ, and every one members one of another. 6 Having then **gifts differing according to the grace that is given to us**, whether **prophecy**, let us prophesy according to the proportion of faith; 7 Or **ministry**, let us wait on our ministering: or he that teacheth, on **teaching**; 8 Or he that exhorteth, on **exhortation**: he that **giveth**, let him do it with simplicity; he that **ruleth**, with diligence; he that **sheweth mercy**, with cheerfulness.* [Emphasis and clarification added]

How are you investing your talents?

_____

_____

_____

_____

_____

What does the King want you to do that you are hiding your talent?

_____

_____

_____

_____

_____

Saturday:

The Value of Your Inheritance

Be encouraged dear Princess, as we finish out our study on being a Princess to the Throne of Grace. With great responsibility, God has also given us reward beyond measure. 1 Peter 1:4-10, *"To an inheritance incorruptible, and undefiled, and that fadeth not away, reserved in heaven for you, 5 Who are kept by the power of God through faith unto salvation ready to be revealed in the last time. 6 Wherein ye greatly rejoice, though now for a season, if need be, ye are in heaviness through manifold temptations: 7 That the trial of your faith, being much more precious than of gold that perisheth, though it be tried with fire, might be found unto praise and honour and glory at the appearing of Jesus Christ: 8 Whom having not seen, ye love; in whom, though now ye see him not, yet believing, ye rejoice with joy unspeakable and full of glory: 9 Receiving the end of your faith, even the salvation of your souls. 10 Of which salvation the prophets have enquired and searched diligently, who prophesied of the grace that should come unto you:"*

Your inheritance with the King of Kings is incorruptible [not subject to decay or dissolution]. It will not fade away and is reserved for you. You have hope in the King of Kings. Princess, continue to trust him no matter what your circumstances of this world. Jesus said in Luke 6:20-23, *"And he lifted up his eyes on his disciples, and said, Blessed be ye poor* [humble devout person]: *for yours is the kingdom of God. 21 Blessed are ye that hunger now: for ye shall be filled. Blessed are ye that weep now: for ye shall laugh. 22 Blessed are ye, when men shall hate you, and when they shall separate you from their company, and shall reproach you, and cast out your name as evil, for the Son of man's sake. 23 Rejoice ye in that day, and leap for joy: for, behold, **your reward is great in heaven**: for in the like manner did their fathers unto the* *prophets."* [Definition added from *Strong's Concordance* and emphasis added]

As a Princess to the Throne of Grace, you are blessed beyond measure. The Prince of this World will try to tempt you just as Jesus was tempted in Matthew 4. James 1:12-15, *"Blessed is the man that endureth temptation: for when he is tried, he shall **receive the crown of life**, which the Lord hath promised to them that love him. 13 Let no man say when he is tempted, I am tempted of God: for God cannot be tempted with evil, neither tempteth he any man: 14 But every man is tempted, when he is drawn away of his own lust, and enticed. 15 Then when lust hath conceived, it bringeth forth sin: and sin, when it is finished, bringeth forth death."* [Emphasis added] Pray that you recognize temptations as lies from the Prince of this World. There is only pleasure in sin for a season.

As a Princess to the Throne of Grace, continue to be moldable pieces of clay that the Father can use. Isaiah 6:8, *"But now, O LORD, thou art our father; we are the clay, and thou our potter; and we all are the work of thy hand."* Just as clay is molded into a cup or dish for a purpose, the King of Kings is molding you into the Princess that He wants you to be in order to bring honor and glory to Him and to advance the kingdom. When a dish is hardened through fire, it is no longer moldable. If it breaks, you may be able to put the pieces back together, but it has cracks and may not be able to be used for its intended purpose. Take a few minutes and let the King speak to you about how He wants you to be more moldable. Write down your reflection of how God can continue to mold you and what area He wants to mold.

_____

_____

_____

Sunday:

Never Forget Your Inheritance

In preparation for a day of worship, ask God to show you areas of your life that need to be changed, submitted to God, and how to encourage others within the fellowship of believers.

Matthew 5:11-16, "***Rejoice, and be exceeding glad****: for* ***great is your reward*** *in heaven: for so persecuted they the prophets which were before you. 13* ***Ye are the salt of the earth****: but if the salt have lost his savour, wherewith shall it be salted? it is thenceforth good for nothing, but to be cast out, and to be trodden under foot of men. 14* ***Ye are the light of the world****. A city that is set on an hill cannot be hid. 15 Neither do men light a candle, and put it under a bushel, but on a candlestick; and it giveth light unto all that are in the house. 16* ***Let your light so shine before men, that they may see your good works, and glorify your Father which is in heaven****.*" [Emphasis added] As a Princess to the Throne of Grace, you can rejoice in the hope of your salvation. Let your light shine, so that others will want to know why you have hope, why you can rejoice when life is tough, and why you can be glad in times of persecution. All of this is to bring honor and glory to the King of Kings.

What did God show me today?

_____

_____

_____

_____

_____

What areas of my life do I need to submit to God?

_____

_____

_____

_____

_____

How can I be a blessing to others or encourage other believers today?

_____

_____

_____

_____

How can I be a blessing to others or encourage others this week?

_____

_____

_____

_____

References

Hengeveld, Nick. *Bible Gateway.* Harper Collins Christian Publishing, 1993, www.biblegateway.com. Accessed between January 1, 2017 to March 1, 2017.

Online Parallel Bible Project. Bible Hub, 2004-2017, biblehub.com. Accessed between January 1, 2017 to March 1, 2017.

HELPS Word Studies. BibleHub.

Rawlinson, George. *The Seven Great Monarchies of the Eastern World, Or, The History, Geography and Antiquities of Chaldaea, Assyria, Babylon, Media, Persia, Parthia, and Sassanian Or New Persian Empire.* J. B. Alden, 1885.

Stongs Concordance.

Matthew Henry Full Commentary.

The Bible. Authorized King James Version. Thomas Nelson, 2001.

About the Author

Mary Jane Clark is first and foremost a Princess to the Throne. She has served along side her husband with teen ministries, college and career ministries, and various other leadership positions in their local church for over 13 years. They have been happily married for 21 years. She is the proud mother of two teenage daughters and a five year old son.